Sussex County, Delaware

Wills
1813-1827

Book G7

K. Louise Planer

Colonial Roots
Lewes, Delaware
2013

COLONIAL ROOTS
17296 Coastal Highway
Lewes, Delaware 19958
1-800-576-8608

Colonial Roots is a genealogy book publisher of source books for the Mid-Atlantic including the areas of Delaware, Maryland, Virginia, New Jersey, Pennsylvania, North Carolina, and South Carolina

Visit our website and online store at
www.colonialroots.com

Some of the features on our website include:
- Current catalog for viewing or downloading
- Surname Index – check to see if your surname is listed in one of our Colonial Families series of books or other books that we carry

Some of our Sussex County, Delaware books include:
- Sussex County, Delaware Marriage References 1648-1800
- Colonial Families of Delaware, Volumes 2, 3, 4, 8, and 10
- Sussex County, Delaware Wills 1800-1813
- Abstracts of the Orphans Court of Sussex County, Delaware, 1708-1709 and 1728-1777
- Some Records of Sussex County, Delaware: The Rev. Turner Collection
- Calendar of Sussex County, Delaware Probate Records 1680-1800

In Loving Memory of

My parents Kathryn and Ralph Lange

and grandparents Lillian and Harry Hamilton

Dedicated to my grandson,
ANTHONY

CONTENTS

INTRODUCTION

Probate records are among the basic building blocks used in constructing a family tree. Wills, inventories, and administration accounts all shed light on family relationships, occupations, property, and financial status.

This volume is part of a planned series which follows the earlier work done by Leon de Valinger Jr. in compiling the *Calendar of Sussex County, Delaware, Probate Records, 1680-1800*, published by the Public Archives Commission in 1964.

This volume represents only the court house recording of the will. Hence it would be advisable to examine original records at the Delaware Public Archives including inventories, accounts, and other records of probate.

F. Edward Wright
Lewes, Delaware
2004

ABBREVIATIONS

dec'd – deceased
Ex. – executor or executrix
Jr. – Junior
ref. or rel. – refused or relinquished executorship of will
Sr. – Senior
U21 – under the age of 21 years
Wit. – witness(es)

1

SUSSEX COUNTY WILLS
1813-1827

Book G7

Page 1. Hudson, Henry. Will made: 14 August 1809. Proved: 26 October 1813. Heirs: Wife Sarah, the mansion during her single life, in case she marries or at her decease to son Henry Hudson: wife Sarah, my Negro man Jacob and Negro woman Alse (wife of Jacob). Eldest daughter Elizabeth May. Eldest son John Hudson, land purchased from Coverdale Cole. Second daughter Sally Reed. To son Henry Hudson tract of land purchased of Levin Willey, also tract of land purchased from Jonathan Hunn formerly occupied by Mary Stuart. Daughter Rachel Hudson. Daughter Nancy Hudson. Ex: wife Sarah Hudson. Wit: Charles Hayes, William Polk, James Johnson.

Page 3. Byran, Nancy. Broad Creek Hundred. Will made 20 December 1812. Proved 16 February 1803. Heir: Brother John Melson. Ex: Brother John Melson. Wit: Levin Bell, Daniel Melson, Thomas Jefferson.

Page 3. Todd, Levin. Will made 15 November 1812. Proved 12 April 1814. Heirs: Wife Ann Todd, eldest son Nathan Todd land where Peter Jenkins now lives near Marshahope (?) Bridge, youngest son Levin Todd, youngest daughter Rhoda Todd, Eldest daughter Salah Hardisty (?), second daughter Anna Morris. Ex: wife Ann Todd and son Nathan Todd. Wit: John Gullett (of John), William Hopkins, Henry Fisher Jr.

Page 4. Marsh, Peter, Sr. Will made 30 December 1812. Proved 4 August 1813. Heirs: wife Mary 1/3 part of my lands. Son Joseph Marsh, Tract of land called "Hatter's Land" adj. Thomas Marsh and James Newbold including what is called the "School House Field" to be divided by a line beginning at Wolpit Branch and running by the edge of Clifton's old field, 35 acres. Son Peter Marsh between King's Creek Branches. Son Matthew W. Marsh, all the rest of my lands. Each of my three daughters. Ex. Wife Mary Marsh. Wit: George H. Hall, John Arnell, Jacob Prettyman.

Page 5. Short, Ishmael. Will made 8 February 1812. Proved 28 December 1813. Heirs: son James, mansion plantation, bounded by Lands of Bedford and Co., heirs of Levin Bevans dec'd, Levin Pepper and the heirs of Nathaniel Waples, dec'd., also silver teaspoons and Family Bible with his names written in it; son John (under 21), land in Nanticoke Hundred purchased of David Hazzard and wife, also Tract of land purchased of Benton Harris in Broadkiln Hundred, smallest set of silver Tablespoons, set of silver teaspoons and one Family Bible with his name written in it. To Woolsey Price, to Elisha Marsey. Wife Elizabeth

Steel. Ex: wife Elizabeth Steel and friend Zachariah Reynolds (Ref). Wit: Covington Reynolds, Zachariah Reynolds, William Pepper.

Page 7. Stockley, Woodman, blacksmith, Cedar Creek. Nuncupative Will Friday, 13 July 1813 - Proved 14 August 1813. Heirs: my wife and children. Negro boy Sampson to serve 7 years then to be free man, George to serve 9 years then to be free man. Hands set 5 August 1813 - John Robinson, Noah Morris.

Page 7-8. Robinson, Rhoda. Will made 10 August 1813. Proved 12 October 1813.Heirs: Nephew John Robinson, sister Molly Hazzard. Ex: Nephew John Robinson. Wit: James Collins, Sally Collins.

Page 8. Hudson, Joseph Coffil. Will made: 13 July 1813. Proved: 24 November 1813. Heirs: Kendal Hudson, 2/3 of lands a part of three Tracts "Buckhill," "Hillards Mistake" and "Cade Addition" and pair of young steers: Lydia Hudson 1/3 of Tracts "Buckhill," "Hillards Mistake" and "Cade Addition" and one black horse. To Grandson, 'William Hayward, a Deed of Land, son of daughter Nancy Hayward, Son John Hudson, daughter Jane Hudson, one beehive, one cow and calf and one Reed [red] apple tree; daughter Sarah, five acres of my land, one beehive and one red cow. Ex: Son Kendal and daughter Lydia Hudson. Wit: Arthur Williams, Samuel R. Williams, Asbury Williams.

Page 9. Hazzard, Lemuel. (otherwise Lemuel West) Will made 8 August 1812. Proved 16 July 1813. Heirs: To Mother Sally Derickson, Negro man Jacob, during her natural life then he is to be free, all the remainder of my estate of every kind to my mother. Ex: Benjamin Holland -(Ref). Wit: Job Jefferson, Arthur West, Mary West.

Page 10. Buntin, John. Will made 17 July 1813. Proved 12 October 1813. All my lands should be rented out and improvements kept up until my sons Walter Buntin and Elijah Buntin arrive at age 21. The money arising from the rent to support my wife and all my children. To Walter Buntin land called "Friend's Assistance," land I bought of Zadock Selby. To Elijah Buntin, land bought of John Hollaway's heirs. The rest of my estate to be divided between my wife and children in 6 equal parts: Wife Elifall(?), Son Marshall Buntin, Daughter Nancy Buntin, Daughter Kitty Buntin, Daughter Betsy Buntin, Daughter Mary Buntin. Ex: Ezekiel Williams, Esq. Wit: John Collins, Benjamin Hudson, Samuel Hudson.

Page 11. Ward, Murphy. - Will made: 27 July 1812. - Proved: 2 March 1813 All my lands to be sold and money arising from the sale applied to the maintenance of Benedict Evans Ward said to be a natural born son of mine, who lives with me. Negro boy Zadock to be hired out. If son dies, what was left to him shall be equally divided between Fanny and Matilda Jester, daughters of Daniel Jester and my sister Charlotte. Carpenter tools to friend Christopher Evans. Executor to pay Charlotte a child of Betsy $10. Benedict to be bound out at age 16 as a Blacksmith. Ex: Samuel Laws. Wit: Tilghman Layton, Thom. Laws.

Page 12. Kinnakin, Sarah. Little Creek Hundred, Nuncupative Will made 8 January 1813. Proved 26 January 1813. Heirs Sarah Kinnsman, daughter of Waitman Kinnakin, my bed and silk Habbit: rest of clothes to Rachel Hasty. Wit. Isaac Vinson, Obediah Hasting.

Page 13. Houston, Priscillah. Will made 28 January 1814. Proved 8 March 1814. Heirs: granddaughter Priscillah Houston, daughter of Liston A. Houston; granddaughter Sally Carlisle (daughter of Charles Carlisle) one cow and ½ her increase, also the bed and furniture where I now lie; granddaughter Eliza Cary, the cattle and all the property bought at sheriff's sale of Nehemiah Cary's; four-daughters Sarah Collins, Elizabeth Cary, Priscillah Carlisle and Nancy Hall. Ex: Son Liston A Houston. Wit: Mary Elliott, Sarah Polk, Jno Cary.

Page 13. Hudson, Lucrecia. Village of Milford, Kent County. Will made 4 May 1814 Proved 23 May 1814. The farm I own in Sussex Co. is to be sold by Ex. Heirs: Grandson William Hudson Collins, bed, furniture and a bureau that I have furnished his mother Sally Collins, now in the possession of Julius A Collins; daughter Cynthia Hudson, daughter Rebecca Hudson. (Money from the above sale is to be divided between William Hudson Collins, Cynthia Collins and Rebecca Collins); son James Hudson, son Robert Hudson, son John Hudson, son David Hudson to receive money collected from the Estate of Daniel Rogers, dec'd. Ex: Son Daniel Hudson. Wit: Samuel Palbatt?, Elias Shockley, Jr.

Page 14. Wiltbank, Cornelius, Lewes and Rehobeth Hundred. Will made 7 May 1813, - Proved: 23 November1813. Wife Sarah, 1/3 part of person estate, also $45 per annum off the land willed son Robert Wiltbank, and $35 per annum off the land willed son John Wiltbank. Daughter Mary (wife of Thomas Metcaff) $2000 of my personal estate over and above what I have before given her, which is to be considered as a bar and discharge of any legacy left her my mother Mary Wiltbank. To son Robert Wiltbank, part of my manor house in Lewes and Rehobeth Hundred, Southeast of a division line to be drawn from Pagan or Canary Creek on the Northwest side of the orchard, from thence a straight line to the corn cribs on the Southeast side of the said cribs on the Northwest side of the Road, thence paneled with Rhodes Shankland's line to the head of the patent line to intersect with John Prettyman's heirs land. Also the Island of marsh in Lewes Creek called "Green Island." To Son John Wiltbank land and marsh laying on the Northwest of division line, including all the lands purchased of Jacob White. To Henry Hudson who married my daughter Nancy $100. To daughter Sally

Wiltbank all the lands bought of Albutus Green. To daughter Hannah, land bought of David Hazzard and 6 acres I bought of my brother, Ex: Wife Sarah Wiltbank, son Robert Wiltbank and friend Samuel Paynter, Jr. Codicil 27 May 1813 Wife to have household goods and Negroes at appraised value. Wife Sarah my Negro girl Nance. In case of the death of my wife before Hannah marries or is of age, Samuel Paynter, Jr. to be guardian. To daughter Hannah 2 acres of land near the "Deep Valley." My Negro boy Robert, to be sold in Philadelphia. Negro Boy Pompey to be free in 4 years. Negro Milford to be free at age 26. Negro Absolom free at age 28. Negro Robert to be free at age 28. Negro girl Nance free at age 27.Wit.Wm Paynter, John Holland, Jacob Hargis

Page 17. Marsh, Peter, of Lewes and Rehobeth. Will made 8 May 1814. Proved 17 August 1814. Heirs: Brother Mathew Marsh. 80 acres to be taken off the Manner Plantation, whereon my Mother and family now live, to be laid off on the West Side. If my brother dies without male issue then to brother Joseph Marsh: Brother Joseph Marsh to have remaining real estate. Mother to have rents and profits during her natural life: Three sisters Peggy Marsh, Sally Marsh and Mary Marsh, if they outlive my Mother to have use of ½ Mansion House while single or maidens, as well as firewood and pasture land. Ex: Brother Joseph Marsh. Wit: Wm. Wolfe, Thomas Warrington.

Page 18. Dale, James. Will made 15 September 1812. Proved 2 August 1814. Heirs: wife Sarah Dale all my land while she remains a widow. Then to my four sons: Peter Dale, John Dale, William Dale and Isaac Dale, to be equally divided between them; daughter Betsy Dale one bed: daughter Tabitha Hopkins, one bed; Daughter Nancy Dale one bed; granddaughter Sarah Banks; grandson William Dale Banks; granddaughter Betsy Banks. To son Peter Dale, lot of ground in Worcester County, Maryland adjoining Jesse Davis. Ex: Son Peter Dale. Wit: Daniel Evans, Robert W. Neil

Page 19. Messick, Miles. Proved _August 1813. My desire to be buried in Asbury Church yard with my name to be written in big letters on Tombstone. Heirs: Brother Covington Messick, my great coat and $100; Sister Leah Bounds a dress to be purchased; my Mother, a dress to be purchased; a cloak shall be purchased for my sister-in-law, Sarah Messick; brother Samuel Messick, my watch and pair of boots. I appoint my father Isaac Robertson my Ex (Ref). Wit Jacob Bounds, James Vickers, Dr. Isaac Robertson.

Page 20. Jester, Elias. Will written: 6 November 1814. Proved 15 November 1814 Heirs: daughter Mary Jester, blue chest and one case of bottles; rest to be sold by my ex, and divided amongst my four children, Mandoff Jester, Outten Jester, Daker Jester and Mary Jester. My beloved friend Jesse Jester and William Taylor, Ex: Wit: John Booth, John Gullett, of John.

Page 21. Taylor, Thomas. Will made: 11 January 1790. Proved 12 October 1813. Heirs: wife Grace Taylor, ¼ part of my moveable estate, son Wm. Woodcraft Taylor, all my land, being two tracts, one called "Fossil's Good Luck" and the other "Scottish Plot" and part of "Cow Quarter," pay 25 pounds to his brother John Benton Taylor comes of age 21, also pay to his sister 20 pounds when she becomes 20. If Wm. Woodcraft Taylor refuses to pay above-mentioned sums, then he is to have only one third of the land and John and Nancy to have the other 2/3 of land instead of money. Ex: Wife Gracy and son Wm Woodcraft Taylor. Wit: Ezekiel Williams, Robert Wildgoose, Edward Williams.

Page 22. Evans, Keziah. Will made: 13 September 1812. Proved 12 October 1814. Heirs: daughter Elizabeth Evans, son-in law Enoch Evans, grandson Stephen Riley Evans, the son of Enoch, granddaughter Peggy Evans of Enoch, granddaughter Kitty of Enoch, granddaughter Mary Evans of Enoch, my son Lemuel Evans, granddaughter Ritty (?) of Lemuel, grandson Lemuel Paty Evans, grandson George Truitt Evans, grandson John Cylus Evans Ex:son-in-law Enoch Evans. Wit: Elijah Evans, Sarah Evans Thos Hazzard.

Page 23. Gordy, Aaron. Will made: 6 June 1812. Proved: 23 December 1814. Heirs: Wife Elizabeth Gordy all my estate during natural life or widowhood, then to my children as follows: Son William Gordy, tract I now live on being part of "Hounds ditch,",,,,,,, one other called "Gordy's Delight," daughter Kitty, daughter Mary Gordy, daughter Jane Gordy.Ex: wife Elizabeth Gordy and son Stephen Gordy (Ref). Wit: John James, John James, jr., Isaac James.

Page 24. Callaway, Clement. Will made: 8 September 1814. Proved: 23 December 1814 Heirs: wife Elizabeth Callaway 1/3 of my estate; daughter Betsy Davis, 1/3 of my lands; daughter Nancy Callaway 1/3 of my lands; Sally Hasting 1/3 of lands; daughter Unice Calloway, three acres;. son-in law Jonathan Hastin; son Joshua Callaway; daughter Mimey Hayns; grandson David Hayns. Wit Robert Polk, Ezekiah Callaway, Ebenezer Lecatt.

Page 25. Callaway, Benjamin, planter. Will made: 3 June1814. Proved: 10 June 1814. Heirs: Kendal Callaway, all land and Manner plantation, wife Nancy Callaway, 1/3 of land during lifetime then to son Kendal. Ex: Guting Lecatt. Witness Stephen Green, Thomas Mitchell, Robert Polk

Page 26. Bradley, William. - Will made: 27 May 1812 - Proved 25 November 1814. Heirs of my brother Joseph Bradley (dec'd) all my lands on north side of the following courses and distances beginning at a post in the first line of a tract called "Addition to John's Folly" running south to a post in the tract called "Addition to Cannons Savanna." Niece Elizabeth Little the remainder of my land. Nephew Joshua Bradley. Nephew William Brown. Niece Polly Wilson. To Betsy Cade (wife of John). All my black people over 25 to be free, those under 25 to serve until they are 25. Remainder of estate to be equally divided between Heirs of Brother Isaac Bradley and Joseph Bradley and heirs of my sister Nancy Brown. Ex: Henry Little. Wit: Clement Rust and John Collins.

Page 27. Ellis, Ellizabeth. Will made 9 June 1814. Proved 5 July 1814 Heirs: son Stephen Ellis, son John Ellis, son William Ellis, daughter Dolly, mentioned Samuel Derickson one cow that I gave him by word of mouth that he has in his possession. Stephen Ellis Ex. Wit: Ebe Connelly, Robert Wildgoose, Samuel Wildgoose.

Page 28. Willey, Margaret, County of Monongalia, West Virginia. Will made: 3 January 1816 Proved: 12 August 1816 Heirs: William P. Willey (Ex) to sell lands in Delaware for cash and give to my four grandchildren, George Willey, Absolom Willey, John Willey and Margent Willey, (Children of William P Wiley) when they come of age.; Margaret Davis, my granddaughter; Mary Davis, my granddaughter; my son James Willey; son John Willey: son Absolom Willey, daughter Nancy Veach; daughter Magdeline Hudson, her sons James and Annias Hudson; granddaughter Margot Willey daughter of James Willey. Wit: Borz Burrows, Carlisle Burrows, Nathaniel Needles

Page 29. Gibbs, Boroughs H., Borough of Hanover, County of York, State of Pennsylvania. Will made: 3 June 1816. Proved: 20 June 1816. Heirs: wife Sarah, all my estate except for $260 in the Bank of Georgetown, Delaware, which in care of the sheriff, to my daughter Emily Jenetta Gibbs. Ex: wife Sarah Gibbs and Nichs Pyles. Wit.

Page 30. Callaway, Ann. Will made: 24 October1807 Proved: 19 August 1814. Heirs: Grandson Nehemiah Callaway all my lands, Granddaughter Sarah Callaway, Daughter Nancy Callaway. Daughter Celeah Ellis. Ex: Daughters Nancy Callaway and Celeah Ellis. Wit: Wm. Polk, Tho. Mitchell, James Collins

Page 31. Prettyman, Thomas,. Will made: 29 June 1814. Proved: 19 July 1814. Heirs: wife Elizabeth, my plantation, lands and person estate, at her death to Thomas Prettyman, son of Wingate Prettyman. Ex: Wife Elizabeth Prettyman. Wit: Jno H. Burton, George Robinson, Levi Hill

Page 32. Lowe, Thomas. Will made: 25 March 1814. Proved: 15 April 1814, Heirs: Brother William Lowe; Brother George Lowe; Brother John Lowe; Sister Sally Beach; Frances Eliss, daughter of Amy Ellis. Ex: Brother William Lowe. Codicil: 25 March 1814: Brother William Lowe to receive any debts due myself. Wit: Wm. Elsey, James C. Linch, Martin Elsey.

Page 33. Bailey, Louder. Will made: 16 February 1814. Proved 8 March 1814. Son Levin Bailey, son Thomas Bailey, son John Bailey, one hundred acres "Rich Ridge." Wife Betsy Bailey shall have all remaining part of my lands, if son Davis Bailey, returns home he is to have the lands of my wife Betsy at her death. If Davis Baily does not return home, my wife can will it as she deems proper. Ex: Wife Betsy Baily. Wit Wm Elzey, John Bradley, Thomas Bailey.

Page 34. Culver, Moses. Will made: 5 July 1813. Proved: 22 July 1814. Heirs: wife Molly Culver, all the goods, chattels and personal estate she came with at the time of our marriage; son Levin Culver, Daughter-in- law Elizabeth Culver, Lovey Vinson, grandson Leavin Culver, all my land, grandsons Moses and Eli Culver; If my grandson Leavin Culver should sell the land the money shall be divided equally between Leavin Culver, Moses Culver and Eli Culver; George Vinson to receive my home. Ex William Cooper. Wit: Wm. Cooper, Willy Phillips, and Joshua Rismner(?)

Page 35. Winwright, Levin. Will made. 9 February 1814. Proved 8 March 1815. Heirs: wife Nelly, all my estate during her natural life except 27 acres of land adj. lands of Joshua King and Lotty Winwright and William Disesons (decd.). to be my son James Winwright's. After the marriage of his Mother, to my four daughters a feather bed a piece. At her death all my estate to be divided between my children. Wit: John Linch, John Hill

Page 36. Wright, Joshua. Will made: May 1814. Proved: 10 June 1814. Heirs: sons Turpin Wright, Jacob Wright, Charles Wright all my lands to be equally divided, daughter Lizzy Wright, daughter Kittura Wright, daughter Eleanor Wright, my daughter Sally Venables children. Ex. Wife Sally Wright, and three sons Turpin Wright, Jacob Wright and Charles Wright. Wit James Twilley, John Gilliss, Josiah King

Page 37. Pritchet, James . Will made: 25 March 1812. Proved 18 March 1814. Heirs: wife Rachel Pritchet all my estate, during her lifetime or widowhood. Have household furniture till the children are 16. To Peggy and Nelly Prichet all the land at the death of Rachel Pritchet. To Euncy(?) Eliss $100 at Rachel Pritchet's death. Ex: my wife and Elijah Phillips. Wit: William Pritchard, Thomas Lowe, Joseph Wilson

Page 37. Bailey, Betsy. Will made 19 February 1814. Proved: 8 March 1814. All the land devised to me by my husband Lowder Bailey, to be the property of my son Levin Bailey, on condition that he pay $100 to my son Thomas at age 21. Ex: Levin Bailey Wit: Wm Elzey, Henry D. Bailey, Thomas Bailey

Page 38. Taylor, Dolly. Will made:15 July 1813. Proved 22 August 1814. Heirs: son James Swain, all my right and title to a Tract "Spicer's Pleasure" containing 59 acres; to Nehemiah Fleetwood Swain. Ex: brother John Fleetwood (ref 16 August 1814). Wit: Hales Spicer, Nehemiah Fleetwood, Sally Fleetwood.

Page 39. Winwright, William. Will made: 17 January 1814. Proved: 1 February 1814. Heirs: Daughters Eliza and Hanna, son Zacheua. Ex: Joseph Betts. Wit: Philip Matthews, Jonathan Betts

Page 39. Cannon, James, Little Creek Hundred. Will made: 19 December 1814. Proved: 20 January 1815. Heirs: son Clement, Manor place and lands adjoining excepting land purchased of Benjamin Vinson; son Ennalls Cannon, land purchased of Benjamin Vinson; to Clement and Ennalls Cannon, my part of saw mill, in partnership with my brothers Joseph and Levi Cannon; daughter Nancy Cannon, $220, if Clement refuses to pay Nancy, she is to receive 100 acres of the land laid out for Clement Cannon; daughter Kitty Cannon, $150, Charlotte Cannon, $135 All my children, Clement Cannon, Hudson Cannon, Ennalls Cannon, Sally Hearn, Allacane(?) Williams, Betsey Melson, Nancy Cannon, Kitty Cannon, Charlotte Cannon. Ex: wife Lucreatia Cannon and Clement Cannon. Wit: Sarah Smith, Wm. B. Cooper, Jeremiah Cannon.

Page 41. Phillips, Joseph, (Dagsborough Hundred) Planter. Will made: 2 June 1814 - Proved: 12 January 1815 Wife Sarah Phillips and son Joseph Phillips tract of land called "Crooked Project" willed to me by my father where the house stands, also 2 parcels out of the tract of land "Pottomack Enlarged" adjoining "Crooked Project;" 2 small parcels bought of my Brother Benjamin Phillips. Daughter Sarah Phillips, land called "Small Hopes" taken up by Philip Hummings, given to me by my Grandfather and mother, all the tract called "Division" to a tract occupied by William Killum, also 25 acres out of a tract called "New Chance" Son Charles and Daughter Sarah to divide tract. Son John Niclson Phillips a tract of land containing 75 acres occupied by William Killum. Daughter in law - Eunice Phillips. Ex: Wife Sarah Phillips, Josiah Truitt (Ref) and Spencer Phillips. Wit: Thomas Phillips, Samuel Gibbins and Spencer Phillips

Page 43. Stephenson, Kendal. Will made: 19 December 1814 Proved: 28 January 1815. Heirs: son Robert Dale Stevenson all that plantation and tract of land I now live on in Indian River Hundred. If he should die without lawful issue, then it should be divided between my six daughters; Nancy, Emily, Eliza, Hetty, Mary and Kitty; wife Elizabeth shall have the use of all my lands for the use of raising my son as well as daughters until the younger reach 16; also to said son one walnut chest which was given me by my father Robert Stevenson. Ex: wife

Elizabeth Stevenson., with Josiah Martin to aid and assist my wife in executing the Will. Wit: Benjamin Prettyman, Thomas Dutton, Wm. Copin(?)

Page 43. Elliott, John. Will made: 9 November 1804 Proved 21 January 1815 Heirs: Son Joseph Elliott shall have my plantation, if he dies underage then to be sold and money divided between all my children. Land I bought for Simon Kollock should be sold. Daughter Polly Elliott, best bed and her part with the rest of the children. Son Thomas Elliott 5 pounds more than his equitable part. My sons Elisha Elliott, Brinkley Elliott, John Elliott and Thomas Adams Elliott shall be bound out for trades when they come of age to choose their masters Ex: my beloved friend Jacob Adams. (Ref) In addition: Wife Sally Elliott shall not have any of my estate only one shilling and no more. Daughter Lizzy shall have one shilling and no more. My son James A. Bayard should have one shilling and no more. Wit: Levin Connaway, James Messick, Betsy Massey

Page 44. Paynter, Samuel; Lewes Town. Will made 14 September 1815 – Proved 9 January 1815 My son David. Wife Meritta, parcel of land, dwelling house, adjoining Cornelius Paynter, and the heirs of Dr. Joseph Hall. To my eldest son Cornelius that tract of land situated in Lewes & Rehobeth Hundred on the road from LewesTown to Burton's, formerly Kollock's Mill whereon Negro Daniel now lives (except the house and 3 acres). To son John Paynter, six acres of Marsh adj. to Peter White's out of the part known as Kollock's Island with a privilege of passage through the adjoining land. My youngest son David Paynter, Daughters Mary Smith and Sarah Webb property formerly of Mary Neal (dec'd) Also a tract of land in Broadkiln Hundred which belonged to Ann Hazzard (dec'd) as purchased by Danl. and Charles Dinge. Son Samuel Paynter that part of his Mother's lands, also a tract known by the name of Cedar Field and part of "Kollock's Island." Son William. Granddaughter Maritta Paynter $130 to be held by my son John. To my Negro Daniel his freedom by the name Daniel Nunitz and bequeath to him the house where he now lives with one acre of land.. I do manumit and release from Slavery Negro Moses by the names of Moses Paynter reserving his service until the 1 June 1813. I lay off to Moses one acre of land adjacent to Daniel. I do manumit Negro Parsley the name of Paris Paynter and bequeath to him one acre. Son Samuel should have the Family Bible. Ex: Wife and my sons William (ref) and David or the surviving of them. Wit: George Parker, Wm. Shankland and John Parker

Page 48. Cook, Mary. Will made 24 July 1813: Proved: 25 April 1814 Heirs: daughter Sally Jones and Granddaughter Mary Lindsey the one half part of a note of hand that I hold on Samuel Stevens to be equally divided between them, and the other one half of the note to be divided between my Granddaughter Mary Parker and Peter Parker, of Peter. Daughter Mary Stevens one shilling and no more. To Daughter Rebecca Parker, one shilling and no more, and if I have any more children living not mentioned I leave them one shilling each and no more. Ex: Daughter Sally Jones. Wit: John Cary, John Parker, Sr.

Page 48. Frampton, Hubert. Will made: 18 April 1815. Proved: 9 May 1815. Heirs: son Richard Frampton a part of my now dwelling plantation, with all the land which I hold or possess adjoining thereon which lies South side of the County Road leading from Crotches ferry to the Chappel branch. To my two daughters Sarah Frampton and Anna Frampton all the whole of the residue of lands I hold and possess with my Gristmill to be equally divided between them. Wife Mary Frampton all my lands and Grist Mill which I now hold and posses during her natural life then to my three children above mentioned. Ex: wife Mary Frampton. Wit: Joseph Vickers, Jno Cary, Jacob Allen.

Page 49. O'Neal, Thomas. Will made: 1811. - Proved: 11 April 1815 Heirs: wife Judith, 1/3 part of my person and real estate during her natural life and no more. Son William O'Neal, one tract of land called "Chance" containing 26 acres. To son, Thomas O'Neal, my plantation "Long Acre" and "Townsend Folly," "Sincerity." Also 4 acres bought of Mr. Joseph Copes. Daughter Rachel O'Neal a residence within the dwelling house that I bequeathed to son Thomas during her single life. My Five daughters: Esther, Isabella, Betsy, Polly and Rachel O'Neal to have my moveable estate. One third part of SawMill to be sold and profits to be divided between my two sons, John O'Neal and James O'Neal. Ex: Wife Judith O'Neal and son Thomas O'Neal. Wit: Jacob Middleton, Polly Carmen, Asa Boyce.

Page 51. Carlisle, Manlove, Ceder Creek. Proved: 1 December 1815. Heirs: Brother Thomas Carlisle, Sister Leah Clendaniel, all my estate: wife Mary Carlisle my personal property her father gave me. Ex: Thomas Carlisle and wife Mary Carlisle (Ref). Wit: Joseph Sudler, Curtis Abbott, John D. Rickards. Mary Carlisle refused Ex. 24 November 1815

Page 51. Bailey, Samuel. Will made 14 February 1814. Proved: 22 December 1815. Heirs: Sons Josiah Thomas Dashill Bailey and Hiram Hiland Bailey all my lands that I own or possess, to be divided equally when they arrive at the age of 21 years, and on half a Saw Mill which was formerly owned by John Collins, also to be divided between Josiah T. D. Bailey and Hiram H. Bailey. To Josiah T.D. Bailey one Negro man named Levin and Negro girl named Mariah. To Hiram Hilard Bailey one Negro man named Dennis and one Negro girl named Eleanor. Out of my estate, $200 for schooling of my two sons. Wife, Nancy Bailey, one Negro woman named Milley and her increase, and one Negro woman named Betty and her increase; also, the remainder of my estate during her natural life or widowhood. Ex; Richard Bradley (Ref 22 December 1815) and my wife Nancy. Wm. Elzey, Thomas Ralph, William Ralph.

Page 52. Collins, John, Sr. Will made 19 March 1814. Proved. 14 October 1815 Heirs: my son Joseph Colinas one shilling and no more; son Joshua Colinas all that part of a Tract of land called "Colinas Chance" which lies on the Westernmost side of a Branch called Cod Creek Branch, that is to say all of said tract which is not covered by the water passing of the Mill now owned by Samuel Bailey and John Beneath: to son Isaac Collins one shilling and no more; son Ebenezar Collins that Tract of land known as Name of "Collins' Dividend," which lies to the North Eastward of the two following lines, that is to say Beginning at a marked Red Oak standing one hundred poles on the fourth line of said Tract called "Collins Dividend" and from thence north forty eight and a half degrees Westerly one hundred and sixty-five poles or to the Ninth line of the said Tract. Grandson John Collins, son of John all that part of the above named Tract of land "Collins Chance" which has not been previously conveyed. To my wife Comfort Collins all the remaining land and personal estate during her natural life or widowhood; and after her death or marriage of my said wife it shall descend to Grandson James Collins, son of Isaac. Ex: Wife and son Ebenezar Collins (Ref) *signed Ebben Collins*, Wit: William Rhoads, Ruben Martinoe, Levin Collins

Page 53. Starr, John. Will made 30 May 1814. Proved 20 February 1815 Heirs: Mary, all my lands and clearings in Indian River Hundred during her widowhood, if she should marry then to be her third only if standing to the Will and after her decease to be left to my son James, if he should survive her. If he should decease without any lawful heir, then to be equally divided between my two youngest daughters Nancy and Harriott; my daughter Sary Dutton one dollar and no more. To my daughter Elizabeth Stephenson one dollar and no more. To Nancy and Harriott Starr, all my moveable property, to be equally divided. Ex: Mary. Wit: Henry Reynolds, Job Reynolds, Polly W. Jones

Page 54. Wattson, Robert, Prime Hook. Will made 13 February 1811 Proved 21 March 1815. Heirs: Grandson William Wattson, son of Bethuel Wattson, all of land. If my said Grandson should die without lawful issue, then the above to descend to William Killingsworth. To my wife Mary Wattson the use and profits of the land above mentioned during her widowhood. Ex: wife Mary Wattson: resigns her right of Executor unto John Smith, 21 March 1815 Wit: Wattson Pepper Will Wit: John Collins, B. Smith, Jesse Aydigion, John Bennett

55. Polk, Charles. Will made: 15 March 1813. Proved 7 March 1815. My whole estate real and personal be sold at public venue. My estate after my debts are paid to be equally divided between my wife and my daughter Margaret W. and my daughter Elizabeth Ann Polk. If either of my children should die

under age or without heirs, then the remaining one shall hold her estate. If both daughters die under age or without heir then their estates shall be equally divided between my brother and sisters. Ex: Brother George Polk, also to be guardian of my two daughters. Wit: John Cary, Clouds(?) B. Warring, George H. Atkins.

Page 56. Sirman, Job. Will made 7 January 1815. Proved. 17 February 1815 Heirs: Nancy Sirman all my land during her natural life, at her death to son John Sirman, my dwelling plantation To son William two men equal to value of Plantation and 29 acres near Laurel know as "Indian Law." Daughter Nancy Sirman $20. Ex: wife Nancy Sirman. Wit: William Sirman, Levin Calloway.

Page 56. Richards, David. Will made 20 December 1801. Proved: 6 March 1815. Heirs: Comfort Richards all my estate Real and Personal for and during her natural life, on condition she raise and school my children that are small. After her decease my personal such as she may leave to be equally divided among my daughters. To my son, William Prettyman Richards all my lands after my wife's decease, if he should die without issue, then my lands to be divided among my daughters. Ex: wife Comfort Richards. Wit: Benjamin Prettyman, Benjamin Richards, Jacob Richards

Page 57 Short, Shadrack. Will made 11 May 1815. Proved: 6 June 1815. Heirs: two sons Phillip Short and George Short, all my land that I now own to be equally divided. Wife, Levina Short, full use of all my lands during her natural life or widowhood. All my moveable estate to my wife during her widowhood then to be equally divided between my daughters: Nancy Short, Elizabeth Short and Mary Short. Son Henry to have his maintenance out of my Estate. Ex: Levina Short. Wit: Betsey Wingate, John Short, and William Freeman

Page 58. Lofland, William Will made 7 April 1815 - Proved 7 November 1816. Wife Phebe Lofland, all my lands purchased of Peter Lindon and that I purchased of Purnel Veach and land my Father William Lofland willed to me, the land bought of Wm. Deputy, Sr. and the land I bought of Charles Williams. Son ,lames $500, also the land he now lives on in Nanticoke Hundred 200 acres. Purnal Lofland's 2 sons, David and Purnal, all the land bequeathed to my wife after her death. Daughter Sally Sharp's, 2 sons, Job and William - $26 each. All the rest divided between son James Lofland, Polly Carpenter, Phebe Conwell, Rachel Carpenter, Amy Sharp and Purnal Lofland. Ex: Son James Lofland. Wit: Jeremiah Townsend, Job Townsend, Jacob Webb.

Page 59. Megee, Rebecca. Will made 7 December 1815 Proved 19 December 1815 Heirs: Sister Elizabeth Megee, my house and land, give to my nefer [nephew] William Megee, son of Wm. Megee, to John Williams, son of Thomas

Megee, to Anna Thorougood. Ex. Brother Thomas Megee (ref). Wit: Spencer Lacey, William B. Ennis, John Davidson

Page 59. Lane, John. Will made 4 July 1815. Proved 9 October 1815. Heirs: Son John Lane the sum of 5 shillings and no more of my estate, son Isaac Lane 5 pounds and no more, son Jacob Lane 5 pounds and no more, daughter Rachel McGlocklin 10 pounds and no more, grandson Lemuel Lane, 5 pounds, when he arrives at age 25, and no more; son Job Lane all my land and tenements whereon I now live. Ex: son Job Lane. Wit: John Carlisle, John Collison

Page 59. Dawson, William. Will made 9 August 1815 Proved 16 September 1815. Heirs: wife Jencey and several small children. Ex: Jencey Dawson and my father Zebdeil Dawson. Wit: William Carlisle, Joel Carlisle, Polly Watson

Page 61. Fleetwood, Abigail, spinster. Will made 22 September 1795. Proved: 26 September1815. Heirs; Lydia Fleetwood, daughter of John, dec'd, 5 pounds in cash: Molly Fleetwood, daughter of John, 5 pounds in cash; John and Parmer Fleetwood, sons of John Fleetwood, dec'd. my house and lots at "Conwell's Landing," near the head of Broadkiln Creek. To Nancy Fleetwood (under 21), daughter of John Fleetwood, Dec'd all my wearing apparel and 50 pounds cash. Ex: Samuel Paynter, Jr. of Broadkiln, Merchant (ref. 9 September' 815) Wit: Sally Paynter, Calda Sddr(?) Samuel Paynter, Jr.

Page 62. Robinson, Joseph, Indian River Hundred. Will made: 2 June 1810. Proved: 23 November 1815. After my death, that an equal and full division should be made of all my lands that I now reside on or own, in two equal parts, by a line drawn and beginning on the western most side, there of and ending on the eastern most side of the same, so that each share shall be as near alike in value as may be. Daughter Ann Robinson and my Grandson Thomas Robinson of the said Ann, the first choice of the one half of all my lands as above mentioned, to be laid off equally, to be divided between them. Grandsons Joseph Barker, Robinson Dashields Prettyman and Elizabeth Prettyman, my beloved Granddaughter, the other moiety of half part of all my lands as above and aforesaid mentioned to be equally divided between them.... But with this final exception, that in case of my said Grandson Joseph Barker should die without issue, his part of my said land herein bequeathed to him shall go to and be the right and property of my Grandson Robinson Dashields Prettyman, and my Granddaughter Elizabeth Prettyman. To Ann Robinson my two Negro men, the one named Caesar and the other Cato. Grandson Thomas Robinson, my Negro boy named Major, Grandson Joseph Barker, my Negro girl named Mary, but in case he die without issue, my will and desire is she should go to and be the joint property of Robinson D. Prettyman and his sister Elizabeth Prettyman. Granddaughter Elizabeth Prettyman, my Negro girl named Nelly, Grandson Robinson D. Prettyman, my

Negro woman named Jane. Ex: Daughter Ann Robinson. Wit: Simon Kollock. Paynter Frame

Page 64. Megee, Bernard. Will made 7 December 1815. Proved: 22 February 1816. Heirs: Polly McGrill, brother Edward Megee, Bernard Megee, son of Polly Mcgrill, Marcus Megee, son of Polly McGrill, Edward Megee, son of Polly Mcgrill. Ex; Nathan Vickers. Major Phillips 22 July 1816 ref administration. Wit: John Handy, Amy. Swiggett, John Gibbons

Page 65. Williams, John, planter. Will made 4 February 1816. Proved: 16 February 1816. Heirs Alefair Williams all my estate during her natural life of widowhood. She shall dispose of said estate to any or all of my children. Ex; wife Alefair Williams Wit: Elijah Williams, Samuel Williams, Mary Ann Melson.

Page 65. Cannon, Arcada. Will made ? December 1815. Proved 8 February 1816 Heirs: Five children, Priscilla R. Green whose part if wish to be deposited with Elijah Cannon, Harriett Cannon, Sally Cannon, Mary Cannon and Catherine Cannon. Real estate to be divided 1/5 part to Comfort Jacobs Green, David Robinson Green, and Lydia Cannon Green children of my daughter Priscilla R. Green, 1/5 part to Harriett Cannon, 1/5 part to Sally Cannon, 1/5 part the Mary Cannon, 1/5 part to Catherine Cannon. My Negro man named Joseph to be manumitted and set free by my ex. after he has worked out or discharges a certain debt due from me to Capt. Robert West. My Negro woman named Comfort shall be free at my death, her daughter Ruthy shall be free when she arrives at age 38. And that Alice, another daughter of said Comfort be sold at Philadelphia. Ex: son-in law Elijiah Cannon. Wit: John White, Albert Holland

Page 66. King, Samuel, Nuncupative will Friday 16 February. Proved: 24 February 1816. First words spoken were in the presence of George Grimshaw, Naomi Johnson, Cornelius Cary and Peggy Cary. "I desire that a debt due me from Stephen Blizzard of 200 bushels of corn shall be given to Eliza Cary, daughter of Cornelius Cary to complete her education." The second and last words spoken were in the presence of Cornelius Cary and Peggy Cary and were as follows " It is my wish and full desire that Elizabeth Cary, daughter of Cornelius Cary shall have a note that was assigned to me by Levin D. Calhoon, given to the said Levin D. Calhoon for 200 bushels of corn by Stephen Blizzard for to complete her education. And likewise, that half a vessel that I own with Cornelius Cary shall be equally divided between my 2 sisters and some wood that I have cut, but can't tell about, but Uncle Charles King can tell." Recorded. 24 February 1816. Wit. George Grimshaw, Naomi Johnson, Cornelius Cary and Margaret Cary.

Page 67. Mitchel, Aba. Will made 1 March 1816. Proved 12 March 1816. Heirs; Brother John Mitchel all my land, 2 beds and furniture, one set of Windsor chairs, one set of Silver tablespoons, one set of Silver teaspoons, also, all the money that is coming by Wm. Clayton Mitchel. To Sally Mitchel, wife of John Mitchel, one woman side saddle, also one loom and all the gears. To Sally Mitchel, wife of John Mitchel and Dolly Taylor all my wearing apparel equally divided between them. To William Mitchel Adkins, son of Stanton Adkins one silver watch, if he should die then it should go to John Mitchel. To Margaret Adkins, wife of Stanton Adkins 4 dollars and no more. To Clayton Cannon, son of Jacob Cannon $10 and no more. To Dolly Taylor, one spinning wheel. Ex: John Mitchel. Wit: Joshua Robinson, William Lockwood, Stephen Hill.

Page 67. Collins, Polly, widow. Will made 13 February 1816. Proved: 23 March 1816 Heirs: son George Collins, brown mare, one yoke of young steers and 1/2 my farm utensils and $8, to my son Eli Collins one brown horse and one yoke of steers I bought of Simpson Hazzard and 1/2 the farm utensils, To daughter Betsy Collins, one cow, new spinning wheels and 2 months schooling, daughter Sally Collins. Ex: sons George and Eli Collins (Ref 23 March 1816) Wit: Purnell Bennett, David Hazzard

Page 69. Dodd, Sarah, Widow. Will made 16 March 1812. Proved: 26 March 1816. Heirs: Adah Dodd, daughter of John Dodd, all and every part of the estate or property that may remain belonging to me, after my funeral charges and debts are paid, except for the wearing apparel which is to be equally divided between the said Adah and her sister Lewah. Ex: son John Dodd .Wit: William Prettyman, Samuel Paynter, Jun.

Page 69. Hayman, Isaac. Will made 17 February 1816. Proved: 15 March 1816. Heirs: son Martin, one bed, furniture and one hat; daughter Polly, the other bed, one Hymn Book and testament. It is my desire that her Aunt Tabitha Twilley should take her and her property till she is 16 years of age. To my son, Isaac Fisher, one chest; my daughter Luceritia James, one trunk. The rest of my property it is my desire that should be sold to pay my debits and if any residue, I should wish my sons Wm. Quinton and Fisher to have between them. It is my desire that William Smith should do the business as far as my wife should, property I have nothing to do with and she is to have nothing to do with what is my estate. Wit: Jacob Elliott, Jerimiah Morris, William Smith

Page 70. Cannon, Ebenezar. Will made 2 April 1816. Proved 10 May 1816. Heirs: son Isaac Cannon all my lands that I bought from Joseph Vinson, also all the land eastward between my dwelling plantation and Isaac's, To son William Cannon, my dwelling plantation that lays to the westernmost of the ditch and to Southernmost of a County Road that leads from Isaac Shorts to Laurel Town; my

Son Levi Cannon all my land that lyeth to the northward of a county Road that lead from Isaac Short's to Laurel Town. if Levi Cannon should die without lawful issue, then to my grandson Ebenezar Cannon; my daughter Leviniah Johnson $100, to my daughter Betsey Cannon $100; to my wife, one bed and furniture, on cow and calf, 1/3 part of my farm during her widowhood. Ex; son Isaac Cannon and Thomas Johnson. Wit Leviniah Hearn, Samuel Hearn.

Page 71. Evans, Jehu. Will made 16 March 1816. Proved 25 March 1816. Heirs; three sons Christopher Evans, Jehu Evans and Elisha Evans all my Estate (property in Northwest Fork, Nanticoke Hundred and lot in Georgetown) all to remain a "ajoint firn in Coe"(?) for the term of 7 years. To daughter Lucrania Taylor one shilling, to son John Evans that went to Sea some years ago, if he should return an equal share of my estate. Ex: son Christopher Evans. Wit: John Evans, Atho(her) Williams, Sarah Messeck

Page 72. Fountain, Zebdiel P., Will made: 23 April 1816. Proved: 29 May 1816 Heirs: Susanna Fountain, Wife is pregnant. If child is not born alive then my wife shall have all my estate. If child is born alive it is my will that my estate be disposed of according to the existing laws. Ex: wife Susanna (Rel) administration should be granted to Ennalls Todd. Wit: Whitefield Hughes, Hudson Cannon, Owen Cook

Page 73. Bennett, John. Will made. 15 May 1815 - Proved: 16 February 1816. Heirs: wife Lizzy Bennett, tract of land where Obediah Wills formerly lived called "Wills's Lott" for her lifetime. At her decease to son Denwood and if he should die without lawful heir begot of his body, then the said land should be divided between the rest of my children. My daughter Ally Hasty a certain tract of land where James Hasty now lives known as "Puzzle Will" containing 130 acres, then to my grandson John B. Hasty, if he should die to be divided between his brothers and sisters, granddaughters Polly Hasty and Hetty Hasty. To son Denwood Bennett, the home plantation known as "Walker's Addition," also 2/3 of my saw Mill and Grist Mill also a Tract of land known as "Mill Lott," also a Tract of land called "Finishing Stroke," also "Turpins Meadow" laying on the south side of the beaverdam Branch and running with the run of the Branch down to Nanticoke River, also a piece of land known as "Prickley Pair Island." Denwood to raise and school daughter Polly and son John. Daughter, Mahala Bennett. Daughter Brittanna Bennett. To son John, a Tract of land formerly the property of Isaac Collins known as "Moore's Privilege" and ½ of "Prickley Pair Island," "Bennett's Lott" 1/3 of the lower Mills both saw and grist mills which are situated on Cod Creek, land called "Mill Lott," "Bennett lott," "Collinses Chance" where John Collins, Jr. formerly lived, and was the property of John Collins, Sr. Ex: Son Denwood Bennett. Wit: George Bennett, Thomas W. Bennett.

Page 75. Thompson, Levin, Blacksmith. Will made 10 October 1804 -
Proved. 14 February 1816 Heirs: Leah my dwelling plantation during her
life or widowhood. At her death to son Isaac Thompson two tracts of land
called "Chancery" and the other called "Thompson's Beginning" all lying on
the south side of the old County Road that leads from Laurel Town to
Tresham's Mill. To daughter Betsey 2 acres out of "Chancery." To son
Clemmon the place where James Sockam formerly lived and also the place I
bought of John Sharp, except the house where Sharp lives and 5 acres,
which I leave to my daughter Lovey Thompson. To son Littleton Thompson
the plantation on the south side of Broad Creek called "Providence." To
Daughter Nancy - 5 acres of "Chancery" next to Isaac Cooper. To Nathan
Harmon, son of Zadock Harmon one bull. Ex: Son Littleton Thompson and
Betsy Thompson. Wit: ? Linch, unreadable, Isaac Linch Codicil 7 October
1808 ½ of part of saw mill bought of John Morris to daughter Betsy, the
other ½ divided between Isaac and Clem.

Page 78. Warren, Ebenezar. Will made 14 March 1813 Proved 3 May 1816 Heirs:
Betsy Dodd one shilling sterling and no more. Daughter Barsheba Donovan, four
dollars, my daughter Sarah Griffith one shilling sterling, son Benjamin Warren one
dollar and ten cents, son Ebenezar Warren, the remainder of my estate. To
daughter Selah Walls, one dollar and 10 cents and no more. Ex: Levinah Warren
and Jobe Donovan. Witness Lodawick Connaway, Zachariah Tam

Page 79. Dickerson, Derry, Nuncupative Will: 1 May 1816. Proved: 21 May 1816.
"Perry Dickerson and John Sharp, joiners in a sain the said part that belongs to the
said Dickerson is ten faddom of Sain and on hundred and seven faddom of Rope
and looks and leads for the faddom of the said and I want it to be rectified for it is
the said Dirkersons desire for the said part to be sold by his wife. May the first day
in the year of our Lord 1816, two loads of slabs and some plank and all the rest of
the said property to belong to his wife Patience, this is the desire of Derry Dickerson
that the said property should belong to his wife. The above was wrote by me on the
day above at the particular requests of the said Deere." Samuel Joseph *(Ed note: This
is verbatim.)*

Page 79. Townsend, William, farmer. Will made 2 October 1816. Proved: 11
October 1816. My blackman named Draper be free at my death and no
longer to be a slave. My blackman Abel be free and serve no more. Ex:
William B Cooper Wit: John Dashill, James Dirickson, Daniel Stewart.

Page 80. Griffith, Joseph. Will made: 20 June 1810. Proved: 17 July 1816.
Heirs: my son Joseph one shilling and no more, son Samuel one equal part
of my estate after it is appraised. My daughter Jane, one equal part; my son
Selathiel one shilling sterling and no more; to my son Selathiel's three
daughters, Sally, Alzabeth

and Janna one equal part of my estate to be equally divided between them. To my daughter Seley 70 acres of land at the south part being part of "Griffith's Lot." Son Moses one shilling and no more. To Moses's youngest daughter Sally one equal part of my estate, Son Isaac one equal part of my estate. My Grandson Hesse the whole of the land whereon I live called "Donohos Chance," Son Avery one equal part of my estate. Son Zoan one shilling and no more. To son Zoan's two daughters, by his first wife six dollars to each one. To my daughter Kirone, one equal part of my estate. Daughter Betsey one shilling. Grandson Evans Griffith Rickards one equal part of my estate. My Negro George shall be free and clear from serving any person. Ex: son Samuel and son Isaac. Wit Joseph Smith, Zippey Clifton, Sally Clifton

Page 81. Lofland, James. Will made 17 October 1816. Proved: 19 November 1816. Heirs: wife Unicy Lofland all my lands in Nanticoke Hundred and Household goods during her natural life; eldest son Nutter Lofland, Sorrel mare called his own and his bridle and saddle; second son, James the sum of $50 when he arrives at 21; third son William Lofland $50 when he arrives at 21; fourth son Elias $50 when he becomes 21. At the death of wife Unicy Lofland, all my lands to be divided equally between my 4 sons. My moveable estate to be divided equally between my 6 daughters: Peggy Lofland, Anna Lofland and Unicey Lofland, Elisea Lofland, Amellea Lofland and Nancy Lofland. Ex: wile Unicey Lofland. Wit: John Carlisle, Fisher H. Willis

Page 82. Tindal, Samuel, Sr. Will made 22 November 1816, Proved: 10 December 1816. Heirs: Son Purnal Tindal tract of land called "Addition to Liberty" containing 279 acres. Negro man Cuff to be free at my death and I give to him my cart and oxen. My Negro girl Febea to be free at 28 years of age. The residue of my personal estate to be divided equally between all my children named Levinah Connaway, Hannah Messick, Nancy Jefferson, Sarah Linch, Purnal Tindal, Holland Connaway, Nica Jefferson, Lovey Harris, Betsey Barr and Minos Tindall. I also exempt 40 feet square of ground, for a burial yard where it now is. Ex: Purnal Tindal Wit: Josiah Marvel, Eli Carpenter.

Paw 83. Mitchell, John, Broad Creek Hundred. 26 May 1815 - Proved 6 December 1816. Heirs: wife Rhoda all my real estate during her natural life, subject to the following provisions; all my black people are to be free at the following times; Delia and Hannah at the time of my death, Benjamin 1818, Rachel 1823, Daniel 1826, Isaac 1828 and Abraham 1831 on the first day of the several years or sooner if wife Rhoda so to free them. If my wife should die before these dates I empower Manaen Bull to find a good "Master" for them. Negroes are to receive land near W. Uriah Short's land. Wife to sell lots near Laurel to pay off debts. If any is left then to Andrew McKain, a son of my sister Rebecca and John Mitchell son of Robert. Ex: Wife Rhoda Mitchell. Wit: Manaen Bull,

Robert Windsor, Solomon Short. Codicil: 2 November 1816 The land of Andrew McKain and John Mitchell, shall now be divided between Andrew McKain, John Mitchell and Andrew Mitchell. Wit: Severign Bonnewell, Peter Hancock.

Page 85 Willey, Solomon Will made 8 January 1816 - Proved 10 December 1816. Heirs, wife Nelly, all my improved lands, with house and orchard that is on the westward and southward of the Connell afd. To the Connell Gate and fence, therewith the cross fences across the plantation toward "Thoroughgood's Savannah." After her death to daughters Margery P. Willey and Polly Willey. Son John Willey, land called "Confusion" it being a part of "Cypress Swamp." To my son Phillip Willey, land where he now lives, that intersects with the Outton line. I give and bequeath to my daughters Nancy Watson, Nelly Thoroughgood, Margery P. Willey and Polly Wiley the rest of my lands. Ex: Son James Wiley. Wit: James Webb, Elizabeth Thompson, Lovey L. Newbold Webb.

Page 86 Cord, Jane. Now in the 83rd year of my age. Will make. 4 June 1815 - Proved 17 December 1816. Heirs: daughter Sarah Cord - the full balance of debt owed to her be paid to her. Balance of my Goods and Chattels I give and devise to my four daughters, Sarah, Jane, Elizabeth Cord and Ann Robbins. I give to Sarah and Ann their dividends to be at their own disposal; Jane and Elizabeth's to be in the hands of my son-in-law David Robbins and his wife Ann Robbins to be prudently advanced to them as the occasions may arise. Ex: David and Ann Robbins. Wit: Isaiah Rowland, Tabitha B. Moore, Mathias Smith.

Page 87. Wright, Jacob, Dorchester Co., State of Maryland. Will made 17 April 1818 - Proved 18 May 1818. Heirs: son Nathan Wright, one dollar and no more, but in the case that the said Nathan Wright, shall pay up a sum of money which I am security for to my brother Isaac, without injuring my own estate then it is my will and desire that he the said Nathan Wright shall come in share and share alike with my other children as hereafter mentioned. Son Levin Wright one dollar and no more. Daughter Sina Handy (wife of Trustin Handy). To My wife Elizabeth Wright Negro woman Leah, now living in Seaford, Sussex County, State of Delaware, during her natural life and at her death to be free. Out of my estate proceeds are to raise and school my two youngest children Jerimiah C. Wright and Mary H Wright for the term of one year each. To my wife's daughter Susanna Fountain one Negro girl named (unreadable) at Susanna's death to go to Zebdial Fountain, son of Susanna, but if Zebdail dies before his mother than Negro girl to go to my daughter Peggy Wallace (wife of Henry Wallace). The remainder of my estate to my children: Nathan Wright, Edward Wright, Elizabeth Vickers, Nancy Willin, Peggy Wallace, Henry Wright, Constant C. Wright, Lewes N. Wright, Heremiah C. Wright and Mary H, Wright. Ex; Son in law Arthur

Willin and wile Elizabeth Wright. Wit: Isaac Wright, Joseph Douglas, William Wright of J.

Page 89. Layton, William. Will made 18 November 1816. Proved 7 January 1817. To wife Nancy, the use of all my lands, being part of 2 tracts called "Holland's Adventure" and "Dubbleton" at her disposal until son Ebe Layton arrives at age 21. Son Robert (U21) my home place. If wife marries, sons should have guardian in order to keep the lands. Wife Nancy, personal property, at her death to my three daughters: Nancy, Lovey and Merriday. To my daughter, Shaday Hitchens, - I shilling. Ex: Wife Nancy Layton.

Page 90. Price, George. Will made 20 December 1816. Proved: 3 January 1817. Heirs: Wife Mary 295 acres of land and 1/2 lying in Somerset: Co., Maryland and on the South side of Wicomico River, during her natural life or widowhood After her death or marriage to be equally divided among my eight children Usua, Peggy Riggin, John, Joseph, Nelly, George and Robert and Benton Price. Ex: Mary Price. Wit: Samuel Williams, John James. Elgit Lank

Page. 90. Boyce, Asa. Will made 21 March 1817 - Proved 28 March 1817. To my wife Mary Boyce all the lands that I possess to raise and school our children Francis and Margaret Boyce. At her death the land to be equally divided between the two children. The Vessel which Silas Boyce and myself are building be completed and should be sold and my share given to my wife and children. The land procured for the building the vessel of Warren Jefferson should be paid out of the proceeds of the sale of the vessel. Ex: Mary Boyce. Wit Warren Jefferson, Milly Carmean, and Sally Callaway.

Page 91. Baker, James. Will made 27 February 1808. Proved 31 January 1817. Heirs: son Jemmey Baker all my land called "Burnt Savannah," being my home plantation. Also all my moveable estate at the decease of my wife Ann. Son Purnal Baker, one shilling; daughter Terrasey Smith, one shilling; daughter Nancy Wright, one shilling. Ex: Wife Ann Baker and son Jemmey Baker. Wit: John Moore, Gilley Moore, Russell Baker

Page 92 . Marvel, Joseph Will Made: 14: March 1817. Proved: 15 April 1817. Heirs: all my lands and Mill to my three sons John R. Marvel, Job Marvel and Joseph Marvel, to be equally divided at age 21. If any of my sons should decease not having lawful begotten heirs of his body, I devise that the said land and mills to my Surviving son or sons. Daughters Lewpinkster Marvel and Susanna Marvel, all my personal estate. Ex. Wife Mary. Wit: Philip Marvel, Adam Marvel.

Page 98. Truitt. John. Will made: 8 May 1817. Proved: 22 July 1817. Heirs: wife Ann 1/3 part of my real and personal estate during her natural life, at her desease to be divided equally between my sons Zadock Truitt and Walter Truitt,. To my sons, Walter Truitt and Zacock Truitt and my two daughters Nancy and Jane Truitt. Tract of land call "Truitt's Choice," 204 acres, adjoining lands of Curtis Shockley, also the tract of land being the place where I now live adjoining the heirs of George Rickards containing 138 acres, the place I purchased from James Hickman. To daughter, Rachel Murphy, $30. To daughter Elizabeth Poynter $30, To daughter Ruth Smith $30 Ex: sons Walter Truitt and Zadock Truitt. Wit: Samuel Ratcliff, Nancy Townsend, Sally Warren.

Page 94. Reed, Mary. Widow. Will made: 1 June 1812. Proved: 23 April 1817 Heirs Daughter Jane Hart five shillings; son Abram Reed five shillings; grandson Samuel Reed five shillings; grandson Robert Gibson five shillings; granddaughter Mary Donovan, the wife of Peter Donovan, five shillings; granddaughter Mary Donovan, wife of Eli Donovan, five shillings; granddaughter Nancy Reed, wife of Donovan Reed late Nancy Pennwell, five shillings; granddaughter Nancy Reed, five shillings; to Rhoda Reed, daughter of James Reed, Jun., Five shillings; granddaughter Rhoda Gibson, five shillings; daughter Lidda Fowler the tract of land where I now live and the Tract of land I bought of John Riley ... she is to take care of and maintain my daughter Elizabeth Reed; Any remaining part of my estate to my daughter Lidda Fowler. Ex: Lidda Fowler. Wit: Jesse Dutton Sr., Jesse Dutton, Jr.

Page 95. Hollis, Sylva. Will made: 27 June 1817. Proved: 29 July 1817, Heirs: sister Lova Hollis, one Negro girl call Maryasa. Remainder of my estate to be equally divided between, Demard Hollis, Pegga Hollas (now Pegga Henness(?)), Zadock Hollis, William Hollis, Nancy Hollis and Hinson Hollis. Ex: Brother- in-law, Wm. Hollis. Wit: John Hollis, Joseph Gray.

Page 95. Moore, Charles. Will made: 22 April 1817. Proved: 31October 1817. Heirs: Elijah Robertson Moore, my dwelling plantation and all my lands adjoining thereto, except one hundred acres which I leave to my son, Lauther Layton Moore, also my still. Elijah Robertson Moore to support his four youngest sisters until the age of 12, also to Elijah R. Moore one Negro man named Laepool and one Negro woman named Phillips. To son Charles Westley Moore tract of land deeded to me by Isaac Hitch and wife, also $300 cash, also my blacksmith tools; to Lauther Taylor Moore 100 acres of land to the Eastward of my plantation including the plantation, whereon Ephraim Waller did formerly live and to be laid off to the best advantage to "soot" the plantation. My two houses and lots in Laurel Town to be sold and the money to be equally divided between my four daughters, Polly Moore, Nelly Rider Moore, Betsey Idalit Moore and Milly Williams Moore. My two sons, Charles Westley Moore and Louther Taylor Moore should be bound out to trades, Charles, a Blacksmith and Louther, to a carpenter at the age of 16. I give to my daughter Hetty Charity Moore $400 cash.

Ex: Elijah Robertson Moore (Refused 29 October 1817) and my brother Levin Moore and William. Moore, Jr. Wit: Thomas Collins, Isaac Moore of Js., Betsey Drane

Page 97. Hall, William Jordan. Will made: 7 May 1805. Proved: 15 May 1817. Heirs; my daughter Peggy Harris, one black walnut tea table, one dollar and no more. My daughter Polly Dales, $300. To son Lemuel Hall all the rest of my estate. To my wife Sally, the use of 1/3 of my estate. Ex: Wife Sally Wit: Benjamin Holland, David Hall, Eliza Hall.

Page 97. Robinson, Ann, Hundred of Indian River. Will made 7 March 1817. Proved 24 Jun 1817. Heirs: son Thomas Robinson all my Estate after my debts (?) be paid as afsd both real and personal, except my Negroes, to him during his natural life, but at his death to be equally divided between his children that he has then living by his present wife Sarah.; son Thomas Robinson all my Negros to him his heirs assigns forever. Ex: son Thomas Robinson. Wit: Robert Morris, David Marvel.

Page 98. Lofland, Gabriel, of Cedar Creek Hundred. Nuncupative Will Thursday 19 June1817. Proved 25 June 1817 I want my Brother Stephen and my Sister Sally to have all my estate to be divided equally between them. "I want my Brother Stephen to settle my business." As witnesses our hands this 23 June 1817 Purnal Lofland, Phebe Lofland

Page 99. Bradley, Joshua. Will made: 3 November 1817. Proved: 18 November 1817. All my property real and personal shall be sold and the proceeds to be equally divided between my wife and my son John Caary Bradley and the child with which my wife is now pregnant. Ex: Wife Eliza Bradley and John Cary, jointly. Wit James Ewing, Lucretia Fowler

Page 99. Draper, John. Will made: 21 January 1815. Proved: 17 December 1817. Heirs: William Draper Lofland, son of Heavlo Lofland and Nehemiah Draper Ales Welsh son of Sarah Welsh all my whole estate both real and personal to be equally divided. If either one should die before age 21, it is to go to the surviving one, if both should die before 21, it should be equally divided between the children of Heavlo Lofland. The house and lot of mine at the Federal Cross Roads should be sold at public sale on a credit of four years given to the purchaser. Heavlo Lofland should have all my wearing apparrel. Ex: John Collins. Wit: .James Ward, John Johnson.

Page 100, Hickman, Nicholas Will made: 31 March 1817. Proved 10 June 1817 Heirs: wife Mary all my land during her life. At her death the land should be divided equally between Nancy Hickman, Levy Hickman and Miriam Hickman.

To Michael Hickman Children, one shilling; Isaac Hickman, one shilling; Roger Hickman, one shilling; daughter Eleander Gullett, one shilling; Jacob Hickman, one shilling; John Hickman, one shilling; Mary Pary one shilling; Nicholas Hickman one shilling; Sally Hickman one shilling; Zachariah Hickman one shilling. Ex: wife Mary Hickman Wit. John Booth, Ezekiel Gullett, John Hickman.

Page 101. Riggs, Levi Will made: 9 February 1817. Proved: 8 March1817. Heirs; wife Elizabeth Riggs 1/3 of my real estate during the term "of her Mortal Life"; two sons Hiran and David Riggs the remaining 2/3. The 1/3 willed to my wife, at her death to go to my two sons. Ex: wife Elizabeth Riggs. Wit: Saml Chichester, John Tatman, James Tatman

Page 102. Hurley, Charles Will made: 13 August 1817. Proved: 4 November 1817; To Stansbury Smith; Wife 1/3 part of my land and 1/3 of my estate; to daughter Elizabeth Williams, 1/3 part of personal Estate; son Burton and the land I hold for him and 1/3 part of personal estate. Ex: wife and son Burton. Wit: Geo. Hazzard, Shad. Robenson.

Page 102. Morgan, Elijah. Will made: September 1813. Proved: 3 December 1813 Heirs: son William Morgan, five shillings; son Jacob Morgan all the real estate that I own or belongs to me, that is the farm and the land adjacent the farm, also the Island that I purchased of John Lord (dec'd) If I should die before the three youngest of my children receive their schooling: Elijah, Lowrensey Dow, Francis Asbury, it is my will that Jacob provide 8 months schooling to a good teacher for each. Residue of estate between all my children: Westley Morgan, Jacob Morgan. Maggy Morgan, Azepy Morgan, Francis Asbury, Lowrensey Dow Morgan and Elijah Morgan. To my wife Hessa Morgan 1/3 of my estate during her natural life then at her death to the above. Ex: son Jacob Morgan. Wit: John Houston, Isaac Adams, Hiran Hughes

Page 103. Insley, John. Will made: 25 September 1816. Proved: 25 October 1816. All my lands, houses, fences and orchards be sold to the highest bidder within two years of my death, by giving 12 months credit with bond and Security. My daughter Nancy to have 3 months schooling, also that the rest of my children be sent to school; expenses to be taken out of my estate before any division. Grandson, Edward Ensley to have $24 to be laid out in schooling, Ex: Wife Betsey Insley, she to receive 1/3 of my estate and the remaining 2/3 be equally divided among my children. Wit: John Bloxsom, John Allen, Nancy Layton.

Page 104. Hudson, Sarah. Will made: 3 December 1816. Proved 7 January 1817 Heirs: Granddaughters Sally C. Reed, Elizabeth Hudson, Polly B. Hudson.

Son John Hudson, Son Henry Hudson. Negro girl Cloe to be sold for term of 6 years then to be free and at her own liberty. The money from the sale to be divided between Sally C. Reed, Polly B. Reed, Sally May, Elizabeth May, Nancy May, Rachel Deputy and Nancy Smith: Ex: son John Hudson. Wit Joseph Sudler, Joseph Hudson, Eliza Hudson.

Page 105. Kollock, Simon, Hundred of Dagsborough, 12 June 1816. Proved Heirs Grandson Simon K. Wilson my mansion house plantation I now reside on with all part of my lands I own or hold on the South and South West side of Sheppen Branch or Mill stream, from the head of the said lands at Haslet Cary's place that now is down through the several tracts which this division will embrace and main run of the branch till it comes to what is deemed the head of the pond and then to include the whole stream and pond with Grist Mill thereon and so much of the land as lies on the South East side of the road leading from said Mill to the bridge with the tract of land called "Dry Boots" I bought of Lacey Morris including this piece of Land will join his other Lands across the branch and serve for the use of a Miller and building. These parts of land to my said grandson Simon K. Wilson will include a tract called "Luck's Addition," part of Old Luck laying in Shelies neck with a tract I own called "Long Looked For." With two small tracts I purchased from John Cloer, part of a tract called "Nancy Fancy," including an island in the Branch below and so up with the main run of the branch to the Bridge above mentioned. I also give to the said grandson a small Island of Marsh I own at the mouth of Duck Creek in the river as I shall leave titles and plats of the whole of my land in the house. If Simon should die without issue, these lands must go to his brother James Wilson. To my Grandson, James Wilson all the rest of my land. Ex: Son in Law Mark Greer of Kent County (REF 16 June 1817), and Grandson Simon K. Wilson. Wit: Charles M. Hill, Thomas Wingate.

Page 107. Carey, Comfort, Indian River Hundred. Will made: 7 June 1817. Proved: 21 June 1817. My daughter Patience Clift, my son Haslett Carey, son Eli Cary, son Thomas Cary, granddaughter Letta Messick, granddaughter Hetty Steel. To my afflicted daughter Comfort Carey and demand that my Ex shall jointly maintain her. Ex: sons Samuel Haslett, Eli and Thomas Carey. Wit Comfort Waples, S. K. Wilson.

Page 108. Wilson, Thomas. Will made 26 August 1817 - Proved 8 September 1817. The new and unfinished house situated on the corner of the lot which was purchased by Thomas and John Wilson of Thomas Townsend, together with the lot and Blacksmith shop theron, as the lot is now laid off, the fence next to George F. Williams's to be the division line, shall be sold and the proceeds be used to pay off my debts. To daughter Harriet Wilson the house and lot whereon George F. Williams now lives, also one set of silver tablespoons marked "HW." To daughter Sinah Wilson, the house were I now live, together with the lot and ground contained within beginning at West end of the south line of the lot I sold Joshua Bradley and running with the sames 20 perches, thence southerly course parallel with the road leading from Bridgeville to Unity Forge as far as the north line of the lot I sold James Knowles, then westerly so as to strike the afsd. Northline and with to the main road and with the road to the beginning. To my son, Elbert Wilson, all the residue of my lands and my silver watch. Ex: wife Lovey Wilson and my brother John Wilson. Wit: Jno Cary, William Wilson and James Ewing.

Page 109. Butler, John. Will made: 20 October 1817 - 5 November 1817. Wife Eunicy Butler, all my lands in Broadkiln Hundred, all my person estate during natural life or widowhood. If she should marry than she is to have 1/3 of estate as dower. Two daughters, Jemima and Nancy share and share alike the 2/3. Son Samuel Butler - 1 shilling. Ex: Eunice Butler and Brother Benjamin Butler. Wit: Daniel Hudson, Elisha Holeston, Abigail Holeston.

Page 110. Mitchell, Rhoda (Broad Creek Hundred). Will made. 14 May 1818 -Proved: 19 May 1818. To Henrietta Windsor, cow and calf, bed. Sheet, blanket, quilt, ewe and land. To Betsy Windsor, bed, sheet, blanket, quilt. To James Wiley, walnut desk. To Samuel Wiley, walnut dining table. To James Windsor, 1/2 dozen silver tablespoons. To John M. Huston, 1/2 doz silver tablespoons, silver watch. To Betsy Morgan, glass tumbler and top. To Negro Daniel, Horse, Ewe and lamb. Negro Rachel, mare, 1/2 China cup, ewe and lamb. Negro Abraham, yoke of oxen, bed and sheet. Negro Hannan, Heifer and bed. Clothes to Nancy Willey, Betsy Morgan, Nelly Crockett and Betsy Windsor. Black people to be free at my death. Ex: James Windsor (ref) and James Wiley (ref). Wit. John Derickson, Elizabeth Riggin, Betsy Short.

Page 111. Townsend, Sarah. Will made 15 March 1818 - Proved: 23 June 1818. Son Jesse Townsend - bed and furniture. Daughter, Sally (wife of John Pool) the house and land where I live, then to her oldest child, if no heirs, then to great, grandson Robert Field. Son of John Field. Granddaughter, Sally Lingo. Granddaughter, Nancy Lingo, Granddaughter Nancy Bell. All the remainder of estate to son Jesse and daughter Sally. Ex: Son Jesse and daughter Sally. Wit: Benjamin Prettyman, Lewes Prettyman.

Page 112. Donovan, Abraham. Will made 28 August 1816 - Proved: 8 June 1818. Wife Mary 1/3 part of my whole estate. Son John Ex (ref) land called "Card Place." Son Kendal Donovan, land where I used to live. Son Abraham, land where I now live. Daughter Elizabeth, one Negro named Cleo. 8 June 1818 Mary Donovan will abide to the will. Wit: Daniel Jester, Dr. Job Donovan.

Page 113. Watson, Smothers. (farmer), Will made 13 February 1817 - Proved 10 May 1817. Son Philip Watson, dutch oven, bed and furniture. Daughter Mary, new iron pot. Wife Nancy, to have bed and furniture, all my moveable estate, land called "Seven Lots" at her death or marriage to son Isaac. Ex: Wife Nancy Watson. Wit: John Thoroughgood, John Wingate, and John Mumford.

Page 114. Short, Wingate (Dagsborough) Will made 23 February 1818 Proved 31 March 1818. Wife Nancy - land where I now live, formerly belonging to Spencer Benson, and land bought of Selby Connaway and land bought of my father. At her death to son Leonard Short. To daughter Betsy - 144 acres in Nanticoke Hundred that had belonged to Jacob Johnson. To Sally Short - land formerly belonging to Joseph Wyatt. Daughter Neomy Short. Daughter Prissey Short. Son Hamilton Short - land bought from Isaac Short. Daughter Levinah Short, 68 acres formerly belonging to James Messick. Son Wingate Short - all the land that belonged to Shadarack Short. Son John Wingate Short. Ex: Nancy Short, wife. Wit: Spencer Phillips, Levin Hopkins and Eli G. Smith Note: 31 March 1818 Nancy Short, widow, elected to claim and hold her dower.

Page 116. Wolfe, William Will made 4 July 1818 Proved 11 July 1818. Wife Mary to have all of my estate, if she marries she is to have none. At her death or marriage estate to be divided as follows to children: Reece Woolfe 3/8, William B. Wolfe 2/8, Sarah Morris 1/8, Ann W. Wolfe 1/8, Hannah B. Wolle 1/8. Ex: Wife Mary Wolfe. Wit: Kendal Batson and David H. White.

Page 118. Davis, Robert (Cedar Creek) Will made 20 May 1818-proved 27 June 1818. Wife Mary 1/3 part of estate and Negro lad Frank and Negro girl Rod. Son John - land in Cedar Creek Hundred adj. William Smith binding on Mispillion Creek. To three daughters Sally, Mary and Susan Pitt Davis - All lands in Slaughter Neck, the home place tract bought of Benjamin Riley and Tract bought of heirs of William Davis Cedar Neck. Ex: Mary Davis, wife and Thomas Davis. Wit: Joseph Haslett, William Hickman and Joseph Sudler.

Page 119. Wingate, John (yeoman) Will made 5 December 1817 Proved 22 September 1818. To my sister Laurania Jones all my lands. To nephew Burton Jones, son of Laurania Jones, horse and colt. To nephew Zachariah Jones, son of Laurania Jones, mare, bridle and saddle, To nephew John Wingate, son of Hessy Wingate. Mary Foskey, daughter of John Foskey, bed, furniture, spinning wheel and chairs. Ex: Laurania Jones. Wit: James Webb, George Messick and Mary Foskey.

Page 120. Short, John Will made 29 July 1818 - Proved 25 August 1818. To my Mother Nelly Short (widow) all my personal estate except Negro boy called Tom and he is to be sold. Daniel Short, Gilly G. Short, Betsy Short (wife of Daniel of

Isaac) and Nelly Vent to pay unto our mother $50 jointly or $12.20 each for their 1/3 of my real estate. To Gilly all my real estate, he paying Daniel $150, Betsey $200, and Nelly Vent $400. Ex: Brother Gilly G. Short. Wit: Adam Short and Hester N. Waples

Page 121. Morris, Robert, Will made 4 December 1817 Proved: 9 January 1818 Heirs: Mary Johnson, Granddaughter, one good bed , suitable furniture, four head of Ewes and one heifer; grandson Robert Timmons, my horse, bridle and saddle; wife Polly sum of $25 all the rest of my estate to my daughter Nicey, wife of Ezekiel Timmons. Ex; Ezekiel Timmons Wit: Chas. M. Hill, Burton Morris

Page 121. Boyce, William. Will made 15 April 1817. Proved 5 February 1818 Eldest son Benjamin Boyce 5 shillings, son Prettyman Boyce 5 shillings, son Robert Boyce 5 shillings, son Hosea Boyce 5 shillings, son William Boyce $160 in lieu of a certain piece of land which I was to give him as per contract and no more provided he does bring no charge against my estate, if he does he is to receive no part. Grandsons Noah Benson and Hosea Benson sons of my daughter Peggy Benson (dec'd) the land and plantation whereon William Benson now lives as follows: beginning at marker three pronged white oak standing in the center of the north prong of Cool Branch from thence upward with channel of said Branch to two small water oaks marked in said Branch and from thence up and with(?) until it intersects with John Jefferson's lands and with said land a Southmost course until it comes opposite a large marked pine at corner of Red Oak Ridge, thence across the said large marked pines intersecting the lands taken up by Warren Jefferson called "Jefferson's Last Struggle" thence with Red Oak Ridge until it intersects William Ellegoods Land, thence with said land to the land that Asey Boyce purchased of Seth Griffith, thence with said land to the place of beginning to them and their heirs.... To my two grandchildren Francis Tyer Ellingsworth, son of Leah Ellingsworth and Margat Boyce daughter of Asey and Polly Boyce all my land to the Northward of the line established in said North prong of Cool Branch, the said line and branch to be the division between Noah and Hosea Benson part and Francis and Marget. I now make the division between Francis Tyer Ellingsworth and Marget Boyce, daughter of Asey and Polly Boyce as follows: Beginning at the before mentioned three pronged marked white oak standing in the center of the North prong of Cool Branch thence to a marked pine or corner of the land that Asey Boyce bought of Seth Griffith, from thence a straight line across the plantation whereon I now live, to a marked Scrub White Oak on the North side of said plantation from thence to the land of Isaac Baker, all the Land on the East side said division line and Warren Jefferson and John Jefferson's land, to Francis Tyer Ellingsworth son of Leah Ellingsworth (Dec'd) to him... and all the land on the west side of said division line before mentioned from the three pronged 'White Oak across the plantation to the marked scrub

Oak with dwelling house, orchard and other buildings to Marget Boyce, daughter of Asey and Polly Boyce, if both should die, land on the eastside to go to Grandson Asey Boyce, son of Hosea and the westside to my Grandson Hosea Benson, son of my daughter Polly Benson (Dec'd) Ex: Hosea Boyce. Wit: Wm. Ellegood, Isaac Baker, Sarah Benson

Page 125. Rust, William Will made 24 August 1818 Proved: 8 September 1818. Heirs: to my four brothers: James Rust, Clement Rust, Jerimiah Rust, and Barney Rust all my estate. except a warrant for land which was allotted to me as one of the Soldiers in the United State Service No. 10032, Issued July 3 1817 which I bequeath unto James Rust.. Land where I now live is to be sold at public sale. Ex; Jerimiah Rust. Wit: John B. White, Clement White.

Page 125. Hasting, William. Will Made: 11 January 1818. Proved 11 September 1818. Heirs: my son Elihu Hasting, all my land where I live and a tract of land in Worcester County, State of Maryland called "Townsends Conclusion," Also, a Negro boy called Arthur. Son Eli Hastings, a small detached piece of land on eastside of W. Isaac Hearn's plantation, also one Negro girl called Heriet. To my daughter Elizabeth Hasting one Negro woman called Phillip. To son Levin Hasting one Negro Boy called James. To daughter Eleanor Hasting one Negro girl called Donney. Son Winder Hasting one Negro girl called Lewezar. One silver watch to my son Elihu. Balance of estate to be divided equally between my four younger children. Ex: Elihu Hasting. Wit: Samuel Elliott, Melvin Hasting, Hezekiah Hasting.

Page 126. Bowman, John, Lewes & Rehobeth Hundred. Will made 10 February 1818. Proved 8 December 1818. Heirs. Son Sanders Bomin 25 cents, son James Bomin 25 cents, grandson John Bomin 25 cents, to my daughter Aley Holland 25 cents, grandchildren of Isaac Boman 25 cents, daughter Sally Hadkins 25 cents. I give to my son John Bomin and Eliza Bomin, my granddaughter the residue of my estate. Ex: son John Bomin. Wit: Richard Paynter, Isaac Ricords

Page 127. Kershaw, Mitchell, of Broad Creek Hundred. Will made: 24 November 1815. Proved 15 January 1819 It is my will that all my Negroes named George, Easter, Peter, Sarah, Rachel, Jack, Isaac, Lizzy, Phillis, William, Mahaley, Maryatta shall be free when they arrive at age 21. George and Easter is already free. To my wife Sally Kershaw, 1/3 of real and personal property or estate except the above named Negroes. My Ex shall sell all my real estate and personal properly except my wife's 1/3. From the sale what is due me, should be divided among the above named Negroes as they arrive at 21. Ex Charles Ross (rel) William R. Cooper (ref). Wit: Armwell Long, Thomas Robinson, Covington Messick

Page 128 Harmond, Elie Will made:17 November 1818. Proved: 19 November 1818. Heirs: My brother William Harmon, the house and Lot that I now dwell on, Brother Arge Harmon one dollar. To my sister Milly Mosely children one dollar each. To Jane Street, my sister Ann's daughter 10 dollars To Ephram Harmon, my sister Ann's son, one dollar To Cary Hanshaw. Ex: my brother William Harmon Wit: Benj. Richards, John Rigwah

Page 129. Williams, Charles. Will made: 29 January 1818. Proved: 1 May 1818. Heirs Brother James Williams all my wearing apparrel as his part of my estate, to my wife Charlotte Williams the residue of my estate. Ex: wife Charlotte. Wit: William Wright, Tinley Bevans

Page 130. Davenport, Mary, Nuncupative Will: Tuesday night, 24 November 1818. Proved: 28 November 1818. "It is my wish and desire that my Brother Stephen Blizzard should take all my property and after paying all my just debts out of it, for him to keep the rest" Signed Naomi Hook. Test Watson Pepper

Page 130. Stuart, Jonathan, Broad Creek. Will made 12 June 1818 Proved: 7 July 1818 Estate to wife Feabea Stuart during her life or widowhood, then to my two young sons Purnal and John. Ex: Feabea, my wife and Joshua Stuart, my son (Ref). Wit: John Boyce, Levinia Johnson, Thomas Johnson

Page 130. Morris, William. Will made: 13 April 1815. Proved: 17 February 1818. Wife Lidda, the use of all my lands and moveable estate during her widowhood; Son, William to receive tract of land known as "Rachel Desire," sons James and Mitchell to equally divide "Williams Luck": at the decease of Lidda, son Joseph, daughter Catey Linch daughter Nancy Linch, daughter Sally Morris Ex. Wife Lidda Morris (ref) Authorized son Mitchell Morris, 16 February 1818. Wit: Ebe Campbell, Wm Campbell, Jr.

Page 132. Carlisle, J. Pemberton Will made: 2 August 1810. Proved:13 January 1818. Heirs Son Charles, plantation where he now lives, with all the farm bought of Thomas Laws; to Pemberton Carlisle, son of Charles, all the land where I live which I bought of William Chance, also the land on the West side of my farm that I bought of Jonathan Bryan; Son Pemberton Carlisle land I bought of Daniel Rogers and James George; Grandson Charles Rickards, tract call "Wolfpet Range." Wife Priscilla, bed and furniture; remainder of Lands not already willed namely the Lot at Shanney and the place bought of Levin Willey equally divided between my three daughters Nancy, Polly and Rebecca. Ex son Charles Carlisle and son-in law Joseph Walton Wit: William Carlisle, Boaz Manlove, Eunice Manlove.

Page 133. Tar, Betsey, formerly of Long Island, State of New York, lately of Maryland, and now the State of Delaware, Will made: 7 March 1818. Proved: 1 April 1818, Heirs: Daughter Jane Parmer $150, youngest daughter, Sally Ellegood, all my silver plate and wearing apparel. Remainder of my estate to be divided between my two daughters, Maria Green and Sally Ellegood. Ex: Son-in law William A. Ellegood. Wit Thomas Townsend, Eleanor Skinner.

Page 134. Puzey, William, planter. Will made: 4 December 1805. Proved (no date). Heirs: Wife Betsy, all my moveable estate and 1/3 of my land; son Ephraim Pusey all my lands; son Ephraim to pay my son Stephen Pusey $120, daughter Nelly Messick, one bed. Ex: son Ephraim Pusey. Wit: Philip Matthews, Elzey Hutson, Daniel Willin.

Page 135. Young, Nathan, Cedar Creek Hundred Will made: 26 December 1818. Proved: 14 January 1819. Heirs: wife Selah Young, the plantations during her natural life, also 1/3 part of moveable estate; Brother Robert Young, 1/2 part of the land and marsh I purchased of Joseph Stockley, 1/2 part of the plantation I now live on after my wife's death; Children of my sister Nancy Davis (Dec) namely Robert, Mary, and Sarah the remaining 1/2 of the land and marsh also the 1/2 of my home plantation. Ex: Selah Young. Wit Joseph Haslet, Thomas Riley, Mary Nickson

Page 136. Ball, Levin D., Broad Creek Hundred. Will made: 9 December 1818. Proved: 29 January 1819. All my estate to be equally divided between my wife Nancy Ball and son Spencer Ball. Ex Wife Nancy Ball. Wit: Peter D. Hitchens, Nicy Hitchens, Thomas Jefferson

Page 136 Messeck, Levi. Will made: 5 February 1818. Proven 2 February 1819 Heirs: wife, Elizabeth, the home plantation during her natural life or widowhood; Children Sally, Love, Levi, Amela and Minus; To sons Levi and Minus all land left to my wife at her death or marriage to be divided equally; To Sally, Love and Amela all moveable estate; to son Willim, all the Reyle tract where he now lives. The old house tract of land from the little ditch down to the big ditch to be sold and the profits to be equally divided between George Messeck, Asa Messeck, Betsy Goshen. To son Noah Messeck 5 shillings, daughter Charlotte 5 shillings, grandchildren of Nathan Messeck 5 shillings each. Ex: wife Elizabeth Messick and son William Messeck Wit: Daniel Jester, Jr., William Morris, Samuel Hemmons

Page 137. Clifton, Mary. Will made: 14 March 1817. Proved: 15 March 1819. Heirs: Hudson Clifton my dwelling plantation; Hudson Clifton and Jehu Clifton, my sons, my moveable property; my five daughters my clothing. Ex: Hudson Clifton. Wit: Stephen B. Lofland, Sally Reed, Dorman Webb.

Page 138: Pride, Job. Will made: 26 March 1819. Proved 30 March 1819, Heirs: Ex. to sell all my lands to pay my just debts. Wife Rachel, 1/3 part of my personal Estate; to my children, the other 2/3 of my personal estate. Ex: Wife Rachel. Wit: Woolsey Pride, Mary Russell, William Russell.

Page 139. Wilis, John. Will made: 2 November 1817 Proved 11 March 1819. Heirs: Son Short A Willis $484.50; son Arthur H. Willis, $484.40; Granddaughters Eliza Martin and Ann Martin $100 dollars each. To daughter Nancy Martin, bed and carriage; To grandson John Martin, blacksmith tools; Daughter Polly Spicer, one shilling: Grandson, John Thomas Ricards $100. The balance of my estate, equally divided between my two sons, Short A. Willis and Arthur H. Willis. Ex: Short A. Willis. Wit: John Collins, Adam Short.

Page 140. Brown, Sophia. Will made: 14 December 1818. Proved: 23 March 1819. Heirs: Daughter, Betsey Watkins, $1; Grandson Thomas Watkins (under 21); Granddaughter Writta Watkins, whole of my estate. She is to pay legacies, of $50 each, at the end of 10 years to Grandchildren William Watkins, Clement Watkins, Thomas Watkins, Anna Watkins, Pegga Watkins and Alafare Watkins. Ex: Granddaughter Writta Watkins. Wit Enoch Spence and his wife Rachel.

Page 141. Hemmons, Selah. Will made: 21 November 1818. Proved 13 April 1819. Heirs: Bebbins Morris, son of William Morris $50; two sons of William Morris, William and Hevalo $10 each. Rest of my estate to be equally divided between Polly Riley and Luke Lofland's children, so that Polly Riley should get 1/3 and Luke Lofland's children get 2/3. Ex: William Morris. Wit: Jesse Dutton, Jr. William Morris.

Page 141 Murray, James. Will made 6 March 1813. Proved 12 April 1819. Heirs: son Richard Murray, my plantation called "Daniel's Place," he paying his brothers Soverign and David $50 apiece; To son Milbron Murray, the manor plantation named "Addition" if he pays his brothers Elisha and Isaac $50 apiece; daughter Nelly Murray. Ex: Elisha Murray. Wit Joseph Long, John Long, Eber Long

Page 142. Deputy, Sally, of Cedar Creek Hundred. Will made: 17 March 1819. Proved: 1 May 1819. Heirs: Sons Joshua, Zachariah and Abraham ...estate to be equally divided. Ex: Son Zachariah Deputy. Wit: William Kendricks, Mark Davis

Page 143. Cannon, Esther, Widow of Isaac Cannon. Will made: 17 September 1817. Proved 10 May 1819. Heirs: Son Sylvester Cannon, $10; three daughters Levina Cannon, Hester Cannon, Polly Cannon, the tract of land bought from Constantine Smith, to be in equal division. Remainder of estate to be equally divided between my three daughters. Ex: Levina Cannon. Wit: Thomas Watts, Harriott Cannon.

Page 144. Smith, Hezekiah. Broad Creek Hundred. Will made: 1 May 1819. Proved: 21 May 1819. Heirs: Daughter, Sally Huffington; daughter, Polly Bryan; Son Charles Smith 52 1/2 acres, upper part of "Pine Grove'; to son Daniel Smith part of "Pine Grove" that may lay Northwest of a line drawn Southwest 33 degrees East. Beginning at a White Oak being a border of a Tract of Land called "Messick's Choice"; wife Lovy Smith. Ex; sons Charles Smith and Daniel Smith. Wit. James Huffington, Jr., Lowder Callaway, Thomas Thompson.

Page 145. Johnson, Rachel. Will made: 21 August 1813. Proved: 18 May 1819. Heirs: Grandson, Isaac; Granddaughter Betsy Johnson; Granddaughter Hannah Dirickson, Daughter Polly Banks; Daughter Comfort Evans; Granddaughter Leah Evans; Daughter Sarah Dale; Grandaughters Betsey, Tabitha and Nancy Dale; Son John Johnson, his sons Purnal, Isaac and Sally, Daughter Leah Gray. Ex not named. Wit: Littn Townsend, Ebe Walter

Page 146. Evans, John. Will made: 12 June 1819. - Proved: 21 June 1819. Heirs: wife Eleanor, the land where I now live, to have and enjoy during her lifetime. At her death, it is to belong to my three daughters, Peggy R. Evans, Betsy D. Evans and Eleanor Evans and the child my wife is now pregnant with; Son Hance Evans the several tracts of land in and about Moses McDaniel's. Also, the tract of land called "Isaac Smith's Tract" and a part of a Tract of land called "Carr's Neck" down to the Saw Mill Dam and the house standing in the forks of the two County Roads near the Mill Dam where Elisha Evans, Sr. now lives; Son Lorenzo Dow Evans, the land I recently came into possession of from the heirs of Jehu Evans. Son Gilead in Kentucky. Ex: Jehu Evans and David Green. Wit: Christopher Evans, Rowland Day, Willin. Thomas

Page 148. Huffington, William. Will made. 20 May 1819 - Proved 18 June 1819. Son William Huffington, Son John Huffington, Son Joshua Huffington, Son James Huffington, Daughter Elizabeth Wonnel. Daughter Ann Outton's six children 1/6 part of 26 acres, their mother to have privilege to use the sale as she and her husband may see fit. Part of "Thomas Court" from Jesse Dawson's line on a division line between my land and William Morgan. Purnal Outton is the father of the six Children. 2 grandchildren of Jonathan. Huffington, dec'd, Mary Ann Gunbey Huffington and William Corban Huffington, 50 acres, to begin at Warren Jefferson's line, where Joshua Huffington's land is along "Thomas Court" to William Morgan's land, which is given to be sold to raise and school and support, not to be held until they are of age. Their mother, now Eliza Calloway shall never receive any benefit or parcel of the said land. Daughter Polly Laws' children Catherine and Emaline Laws and James Laws, Daughter Susanna

Hill, 80 acres alongside of mentioned land. Daughter Rachel Huffington - land. Ex: James Huffington and Rachel Huffington. Wit: James H. Baker, Daniel Rogers, and Mary Rogers.

Page 150. Heavloe, Anthony. Will made: 2 August 1818. Proved: 24 June 1819. Heirs: son, Jesse; Son, Edward; Son, Anthony; Daughter, Ester Pettyjohn; son, Stapleford; Son, Rhuben; Son, David; daughter, Jemima; son, Bennet W.; Wife Margaret residue of estate, lands that is a land warrant that is not granted to be recorded by John Russel to my said wife Mary. Ex. Wife, Margaret Wit: Frazier Gray, William Gray, Eliza Gray

Page 151- Nunez, Hannah. Will made 19 August 1816 - Proved 24 June 1819. Niece Mary Train - my property. Ex: Mary Train. Wit: Caleb Rodney, Baily A. West, and David Hazzard. Codicil: 3 gowns, my old clothes, 2 old tables, 3 or 4 chairs, bed and bedstead to go to my late Negro woman Ruth, wife of Cudge Richards, if she is dead, then to her children 25 August 1817 - Wit: Caleb Rodney, Baily A. West.

Page 152. Mills, Jonathan. Will made 6 October 1818 - Proved 17 November 1818. Daughter Isabella Green, all my lands in Dagsborough Hundred known as "Partnership" it being a part of "Partnership." Daughter Sarah Mills, a bed that is at the home of George Green. Daughter Mary Killiam , bed at the house of James Killiam. Daughter Ann Wingate. Daughter Hannah Hanson. Ex: James Killiam and George Green. Wit: John Thoroughgood, Jno. Burton, Robert Frame.

Page 153. Boston, Solomon. Will made 25 June 1819 - Proved 19 July 1819. Wife Sally Boston, my whole estate during her natural life or widowhood, then to be settled by the Laws of the State. For the education of my three sons: Solomon, John and Charles. Their mother will bound them out at the proper ages for a trade or vocation. Ex: Wife Sally Boston. Wit: John Rust and Job Stokly.

Page 154. Phillips, John Sheppard, Dagsborough Hundred, farmer. Will made 13 July 1819 - Proved 7 September 1819. To my mother Leveniah Hopkins, all my land that my father John Phillips, dec'd, left me, until my brother Spencer Phillips comes of age. Sister Polly Wingate Phillips to receive $50 from Spencer for the land. Ex: Father in law - John Hopkins. Wit: Spencer Phillips, Jane Hopkins and Burton Phillips.

Page 154. Dawson, Zebedial. Will made 10 March 1819 - Proved 21 September 1819. Wife Prudence Dawson, 2 acres of land, to have a house built for her by my Ex. in a convenient place and where it will be the least damage to the farm from renting. Daughter Sarah Shaw of Philadelphia. Granddaughter Mary Jane Dawson. Granddaughter Celia Dawson, Grandson Zebedial Dawson. Grandson

William Dawson. Granddaughter Sarah Dawson. Grandson Samuel Dawson. Residue to be divided between daughters Arm Dawson and Mary Dawson. Wit: Charles Todd, HenryTodd and John Booth.

Page 156. Hazzard, Mary, Broadkiln Hundred Will made 28 December 1815 Proved 3 November 1819. To my two daughters living with me, Elizabeth King and Mary King, all my cleared estate, I now possess, real and personal. I give unto my several children and grandchildren: George King, John King, Samuel King, and Winifred King and several children of Nancy Conwell (late Nancy King), and Sarah Prettyman (late Sarah King) and Charles King. 12 1/2 cents each, as their share of estate. Ex: Son Charles King (Rel). Wit: Jacob White and Mary White.

Page 157 Shankland, Sary, Widow. Will made 17 January 1815 - Proved 27 November 1819. To nephew Jeames Prettyman, son of my brother Robert, he was born of Mary Wiatt, all my lands in Indian River Hundred-it being left to me by my father Robert Prettyman; if he dies without heir, then lands to nephew Robert Prettyman son of Brother William Prettyman. I give to Robert Prettyman son of James a bed and furniture. To Lydia Prettyman my long cloak. Set of silver teaspoons to Ann Prettyman the daughter of Jeames. Ex: Jeames Prettyman. Wit: Coard Burton and John Lingo.

Page 157. Robbins, William, Sr. Will made 16 April 1819 - Proved 22 June 1819. Daughter Sarah Card, Daughter Sealey Linch, daughter Nancy Sharp, Son Daniel Robbins, Daughter Elizabeth Parker, son John Robbins, son Joseph Robbins, Son George Robbins, granddaughter Elizabeth Robbins, (daughter of Joseph, one walnut desk at the decease of Abigail my wife. Wife Abigail the rest of my estate. Ex: Wife Abigail. Wit: James P Truitt, James Redden and Lovey Johnson.

Page 158. Shankland, William Will made 25 April 1819 Proved to my wife Mary 1/3 part of all my personal estate. Also one other 1/6 part to be enjoyed during widowhood but returned at the term of 3 months from her marriage. Also all my right and title to a lot in Lewes Town, sold by us to George Parker with the privilege to redeem the same. If she decides to reside on the home farm, to provide a suitable tenement, she may provide a lease of ground that shall not expire until 2 years after her death. To my daughter and her children all the rest of my estate. Ex: Wife Mary and Jno H. Burton, current husband of my daughter. Wit: Jehu Stockley, Esq (age about 32) and John Parker (age about 3,5). Mary Shankland refused executorship 21 Dec 1819

Page 160. Dean, Charles. Will made 27 August 1819 - Proved 1 October 1819 Wife Sally, 1/3 part of estate, then the balance to son Elisha Dean, Ebey Dean, Alby Dean and Peggy Dean. To my 1/2 brother, Benjamin Reed, one bed and furniture. Ex: Brother in law: James Wolliss. Wit: Wm P. Chittaw, William Reed and James Marvel.

Page 161. Adams, Jacob. Will made 3 February 1819 - Proved 17 December 1819. Wife Rachel, 1/3 of all my property. Son Thomas, land called "Delight" and land called "Good Neighborhood." All my moveable property to my three children Thomas Adams, Nancy Jones and Sally Magee. Ex: Wife Rachel Adams. Wit: Daniel Baker and Isaac Baker.

Page 162. Bagwell, Patience. Will made 13 January 1813 - Proved 13 January 1820. To Cornelius Burton the expense he is at in repairing the wall round a graveyard at his house. To William B. Burton, if no account against my estate, all my farming equipment, yoke of oxen, watch, desk, breakfast table, 2 cupboards bed and bedstead, dutch oven, sm. Pot, however if he has account against my estate then the above items are void. To Lydia Burton, 6 chairs, 6 pewter plates, pair of irons, brass candlestick, dutch oven, dish kettle. To Elizabeth Irons, one cow. To Patience Newcomb, large looking glass, 6 silver teaspoons during her life at her death to her daughter Cornelia Burton. To Comfort Parke, oval table, copper coffee pot, then to her daughter Arcady Burton. To Mary Burton, a cloth .cloak. To Cornelia Burton, bed and furniture, suit of curtains, brass candlestick, 2 pewter dishes, iron pot, arm chair. To Maria Burton a walnut tea table. To Isaiah Burton one Silver spoon marked "J.P.B.." To Thomas Burton - all the residue of my estate. Ex: Thomas Burton. Wit: Isaiah Clift, Elijah Warrington, Gideon Burton.

Page 163. Houston, William. Will made 17 April 1819 - Proved 15 January 1820. To Wife Elizabeth, all of my estate. The residue of my estate, at death of wife, to nephew William Houston, son of my brother Joseph Houston. At his death to my wife's brother Joseph Vent. Ex: Wife Elizabeth Houston. Wit: David Hazzard and William Vent.

Page 164. Long, George (colored man). Will made: 4 November 1819 - Proved 25 January 1820. All my debts to be paid out of proceeds of my sons Mitchel and Isaac, which I bought of Levina and Samuel T. Connaway. To John Tindal, my son Mitchel, until he turns 25. To Minus Tindal, my son Isaac, until he turns 25. My desire is that my sons should be free at age 25. Ex: friends, John and Minus Tindal. Wit: Purnal Tindal, Robert Barr, and Daniel Hudson.

Page 164. Brown, Martha, Will made: 19 January 1820 - Proved: 22 February 1821. To my grandson Stapleford Banning - all my estate. Ex: Son William Neal. Wit: Jno Cay, Arthur Neal, and .John Neal, Jr.

Page 165. Carmean, Milly. Will made 19 February 1818 - Proved 11 February 1820 Eldest daughter Polly Boyce. Daughter Sally Benson. Hessy Vinson. Son Higgens Carmean - all my land. Daughter Betsy Carmean, Daughter Nancy Carmean. Daughter Lovey Carmean. Ex: Higgins Carmean. Wit: Wm. Ellgood and Wm. O'Neal.

Page 166 Waller, Thomas Will made 9 October 1819. - Proved 11 April 1820. To friends George and Joseph Hearn all my land on both sides of mill where I now live, George to have two parts and Joseph his brother the other, To friend Thomas Sullivan and Levin, his son, all my lands, rights, titles of the lands where Thomas Sullivan and Isaac LeCatt now live equally to be divided between them. To Betsy, James R., Thomas, Wm. and Patty H. Sullivan all my moveable estate, to be sold and the money to be divided between them equally. To Sally Davis, $120 to be raised of my land and to be paid 20 yearly. Ex: George Hearn. Wit: William Smith, Jerimiah Morris and William Morris

Page 167. Phillips, Richard. Will made 16 June 1818 - Proved 28 July 1820. To son Levin Phillips, 100 acres called "Taylor's Addition" and "Bradley Delight," if he dies without heir then to sons Richard and George Phillips. To my sons Jonathan Bailey Phillips and Samuel Phillips all the remainder of my land. To my wife, Leveniah Phillips, all my crops. Daughter Nancy Twilley wife of Robert Twilley. Sarah Darby, wife of Thomas Darby. Daughter Levinah Phillips, wife of Peregrin Phillips. Daughter Betsy Bennett wife of William Bennet. Ex: Son Richard Phillips (ref) Wit: Jno Polk, John King, Thomas Hearn.

Page 169. Davidson, William. Will made 24 December 1814 - Proved 7 July 1820. Wife Elizabeth Davidson, my land, household goods, after her death or marriage to Daughter Elizabeth Hill, then to her son John Hill, if he dies to his younger brother or sister. Ex: Wife Elizabeth Davidson. Wit: Absolom Rust, Nathaniel Blizzard, Anderson Johnson.

Page 170 Waller, Eleanor. Will made. 20 June 1820 - Proved 8 September 1820. Eldest son, James L. Waller. Daughter Nancy Waller, Son John Richard Waller, George Waller, Thomas Waller - all the lands where I live bought of George Waller. Granddaughter Eleanor Waller (U16) daughter of Nancy. Granddaughter Eleanor Waller, daughter of James L. Granddaughter Parry Ann Waller, daughter of Richard. Grandson William Waller, son of George. Ex: Son Thomas Waller. Wit: Jonathan Waller, Theophilius Nicholson, Henrietta W. Kellum.

Page 171 Callaway, Nehemiah. Sr, Will made 15 March 1815 - Proved 8 September 1820. Son Ebenezer - land where I now live. Son Joseph Calloway - land purchased of William Polk. Son Isaac - land and plantation purchased of

John Goddard. Daughter Sally Callaway. That Ebenezer Callaway keep the boy called Joshua Parker until age 21. Residue of my estate to all my children: Isaac Callaway, Ebenezer Callaway, Josiah Callaway, Nanny Callaway, Polly Hearn, Sally Callaway, Rachel Callaway, Children of Patience Callaway. Ex: Sons Isaac and Ebenezer Callaway. Wit: William Elsey, William Hearn, and Elizabeth Callaway.

Page 173. Hughes, John. Will made 26 August 1820 - Proved: 19 September 1820. Hiram Ex and heir to my estate by paying or causing to pay Whitefield Hughes the sum of $500, if Hiram refuses to pay Whitefield Hughes, then entire estate to be divided between Hiram and Whitefield. Wit George Hazzard and John Windsor.

Page 174. Hitchens, Jarrett, Will made 6 June 1818 - Proved 6 October 1820. Wife Lovey, first choice of bed, to wife and Samuel Benson, son of Sally Benson, my milk cow. Son Shadrick, son Spencer Hitchens, Daughter Sally Waiters (widow). Ex: Wife Lovey Hitchens. Wit: Samuel Hitch, Levin Hitch, and William Hitch.

Page 175. Argoe, Alexander. Will made 24 September 1820 - Proved 7 October 1820. Wife Sally D. Argoe, bed, furniture, cow and calf, pigs, chairs, ox cart, mare and carriage, Also 1/2 part of my home plantation. Son John Argoe, Son Andrew Argoe, Son Samuel B. to have "Argoe's Delight" on William Mill Branch. son Jorden - land in Nanticoke Hundred adj. Purnal Tatman, son Charles, Son Alexander, daughter Sally Davis Argoe. Ex: Samuel B. Argoe and Jorden Argoe. Wit: Joseph Sudler, Purnal Tatman and Purnal Tatman, Jr.

Page 176 Murphey, Hannah (Lewes Rehobeth and Pilot Town) 2 November 1802 - Proved 13 May 1814. I bequeath the moiety or half of my house and lot situated on the banks of Lewes Creek adj. Lands of William Harris and heirs of Jacob Art, dec'd unto my brother Samuel Thompson and his wife Margaret during their natural lives and after their decease, to my nephew Joseph (the son of my said brother Samuel), if he should die without issue then to nephew Andrew Thompson, then to nephew James Thompson. Ex: Brother Samuel Thompson and his wife Margaret. Wit: Daniel Rodney and Sarah Rodney.

Page 177. Walter, John. Will made 4 March 1815 - Proved 15 November 1815. All my property to be sold by my Ex, the money from sale to go to my daughter Peggy and son John. Ex: Ebe Walter, Esq. Wit: Jos. Russell and Abner Coffin.

Page 177. Records, Thomas (Little Creek Hundred) Will made 24 May 1815 -Proved: 24 November 1815. To son Thomas Wiltbank Records, all the lands in Little Creek Hundred bought of John Williams, Jr. and also from Charles Moore. To daughter Selah Records, land in Little Creek Hundred whereon I now live, also "Snow Hill," "Silver Banks" and "Round About" bought of Thomas Hosea-and Wooten Loyd. To my brother Risdon Records $50 cash. To brother Records land "Rabbit Hunt." To Rachel Hitch, who lives with me, one bed and furniture, If my 2 children die land to be divided among my brothers and sisters: Selah Carmean, Sarah Waller, Catherine Turner. Nancy Marchman, Rachel Hasting, William Records, Risdon Records. Ex: Brother William Records and friend William B. Cooper. Codicil 24 May 1815: Joshua Hasting, husband of my sister Rachel, one cow and calf. Wit: Jackson Gordy and John Skelly.

Page 179. Warrington, Hester (Rehobeth). Will made: 27 June 1815 - Proved September 1816. To daughter Cornelia Little, the place where I now reside, Also all my wearing apparel, she disposing to my granddaughter, crockery ware, silver (except one tankard in possession of my son Thomas), Also to daughter Cornelia and granddaughter Hester Warrington, one bed each. To son Thomas Warrington, the residue of my estate and remainder of the house and lot at the death of my daughter Cornelia Little. Also, to Thomas, the silver tankard in his possession, at his death to his eldest child, male or female. Ex: Sons Thomas Warrington and John Little. Wit: Wm. Shankland and Joseph Marsh

Page 180. Hood, Mary. Will made 7 September 1816 - Proved: 29 October 1816. To son John Hood - Negro man Thomas until he arrives at age 28. Granddaughter, Jane Perry, a cow and calf and looking glass. Ex: Son John Hood. Wit: Woolsey B. Cary and Samuel Ennis.

Page 181 Lecatt, Gustaves, Will made. 22 February 1815 - Proved 9 May 1817. Wife Elender - all my real and personal property. Lands to sons Gustaves, Benjamin, Ebenezer and Shadrack's two sons. The moveable property -1/2 to wife and 1/2 (to be equally divided between) Nehemiah Lecatt's son Elijah and Shadrack Lecatt's son John. Wit: Samuel Elliott, Nancy Elliott and Betsy Elliott.

Page 181 Argo, Joseph, Sr. (Mispillion Neck, Kent Co., Delaware) Will made 28 November 1818 - Proved 30 January 1819. To granddaughter Mary Houston Argo $50. To daughter Jessisiah Webb $50. Rest of estate to be equally divided between wife Sarah Argo and my son John Argo. Ex: Sarah Argo, wife, and son Alexander Argo. Wit: Cornelius Hane and Mary Argo.

Page 182. McCracken, John (Town of Lewes) Will made 9 July 1818 - Proved 6 February 1819. To daughter Elizabeth Truscon heir/heirs, house, furniture or whatever is left after my debts are paid. Wit: Daniel McCollister and Henry McCracken.

Page 183. Bryan, Mary Ann. (Town of Lewes) Will made 12 July 1811 - Proved 22 February 1820. To my relatives Ann Clampett, (wife of John), Isaac Hall,

Lydia McKemmy, Thomas Hill 50 cents each. To friend Elizabeth Rodney, all the residue of my estate. Ex: Caleb Rodney and Elizabeth Rodney. Wit: Wm. West and John M. West.

Page 183. Rodney, Thomas. (Town of Lewes) Will made 1 September 1817 - Proved 29 May 1820. To brothers, Daniel, Caleb, John Rodney, all my real estate And Trust and special confidence that will immediately after my decease to make division and disposition of the same as to them or a majority if they may seem equitable and right to the laws of the state, subject to two conditions. 1. That my daughter Mary while she continues under coverture or married to her present husband Wm. Robinson, should have no part of my estate, in case she should die before her afsd husband and leave issue by him it is my desire, that my trustees shall hold her part of my estate for her heirs until they arrive at lawful age. 2. That if all my children and grandchildren die without issue that all that is left to them go back to the trustees and their heirs. Wit. Bailey A. West and Thomas Bell

Page 184. Cannon, Mary (widow) (Broad Creek Hundred). Will made. 2 September 1816 - Proved 13 September 1816. My Negro man Harry to be hired out till he works our $125, if he does he shall be free. Son Joseph B. Cannon. $59. Sons and Daughters: Levina Cannon, Betsy Cannon, Clayton Cannon and Jacob Cannon should be raised and schooled out of my estate, The remainder of my estate to children: Joseph B. Cannon, Burton Cannon, Cyrus Cannon, Gibson Cannon, Levina Cannon, Betsy Cannon, Clayton Cannon and Jacob Cannon. Ex: Josiah Truitt and Thomas Johnson. Wit: Spencer Phillips, Neomy Stockley, and Levina Truitt.

Page 185. Warrenton, Luke. Will made 15 March 1815 - Proved 12 February 1821. Wife Nelly - 15 acres of land where I now dwell, also all my moveable property to her and her heirs begotten by me and if no heir surviving me then to my Eldest son Robert Warrenton. Wit: John Huffington, Edmund Johnson, George Warrington.

Pages 186 and 187 are blank; pages 188,189,190 are Missing pages from Will Book

Page 191. Morris, Lacey. Will made: 9 July 1814. Proved: 14 November 1820. Heirs: Wife Tabitha, 1/3 part of my estate during her widowhood and no more. Son Ephraim Morris, land where he now lives called "Rich Island" and fifteen acres I bought of John Morris adjoining it, during his life and after his death the aforesaid land to go to my Grandson Lacey Morris, son of the afsd. Ephraim. To my Grandchildren, Hessy and Burton (daughter and son, of my son Thomas Morris), all the following land, beginning at a white oak corner standing near the road and running a north course to the old pond and including all the land I

40

bought of Nathan Frame, equally divided between them. Son Robert, all the land whereon I now live and all the adjoining lands to me not already disposed of. To my daughter, Sarah Stephenson, one ewe and lamb, double counterpane and no more. To my daughter Polly Green, one cow I lent her, one ewe and lamb and no more. Ex: Son Robert Morris. Wit: Joram(?) Griffith, Aaron Marvel, and Purnal Jones

Page 192. Ross, Robert. Will made: 6 November 1820. Proved: 21 November 1820. Heirs: wife Mary Ross to possess my entire estate during her natural life as a widow, if she marries then my farm and 2/3 of my personal estate, to my adopted son Risdon R. Cannon, lawful son of Thomas and Sarah Cannon. Wife Mary Ross shall possess my house and lot in Bridgeville. After her death to Risdon R. Cannon. Ex: Wife Mary Ross and Risdon R. Cannon. Wit: Jno Cary, William M. Morris, Elijah Victor.

Page 192. Ross, Gibson. Will made: 17 March 1815. Proved: 24 November 1820. Heirs: Son William Ross, the plantation farm, whereon I now live, to be laid off by a line beginning at the East end of a division line between Harriott Ross and myself and to run from thence to the lane leaving the fence about six perches to the Eastward, from thence to Hughlets Bounder at a fording place in Iron mine Branch and from there with said branch and mill pond to my outside line in great branch, including all my land lying North of Iron Mine Branch; Son, Henry Ross, all my land lying South of Iron Mine Branch to its outside metes and bounds together with one equal 1/2 part of Iron Mine Branch and Mill near thereon; Son Charles Ross, Tract of land call "Double Purchase," one other Tract called "Fragment" also one hundred and four and 3/4 acres I purchased of William G. Tilghman; Son John Ross, shall hold and possess all that tract of land I hold in right of my wife together with 17 and 3/4 acres of land adjoining which I took up, and should anyone one of my children, when they arrive of age refuse to release to John all then- right and claim to the aforesaid land I give to John $100 out of each one's part of my estate, so refusing; Daughter Sarah Ross, $50 and one set silver tablespoons marked "GR." All my person estate to be equally divided between my four daughters; Sarah Ross, Nancy Ross, Mary Ross, and Margaret Ross. Ex: Son-in-law Roger Adams. Wit Dr. John Cary, Sally Coalbourn, Clement Ross.

Page 194. Brereton, Thomas. Will Made: 6 December 1819. Proved: 28 December 1820. Heirs: Grandson James Aydelott Brereton, my plantation, in the forks of Herring Creek; To my sons, David and Daniel Brereton, the plantation whereon I now dwell, which I purchased of William Russell (except two acres and the House where my Negro man Cudjo now lives); Wife Patience; daughter Patience, the wife of Samuel Brereton; Granddaughter Nancy Hazzard who now lives with me $50; To my Negro man Cudjo his freeedom, together with two acres

Page 202. Coulborn, Thomas. Will made 10 September 1818. Proved: 6 March 1821. Heirs: Eldest son, Jeremiah, the lands where he now lives; son Michael, land where he now lives, with the farm I bought from Edward Cannon; Son Thomas Coulborn the home farm, where I live, with the farm where he now lives; daughter Anna, the house and 2 acres where Elijah Libbe lives; Grandchildren, Nancy Goslin and John Goslin, heirs of my daughter Elizabeth Goslin; Wife Catherine Coulborn; daughter Sally Cannon wife of Levi Cannon. Ex Sons Jeremiah and Michael Coulbourn, Wit: Joseph Cannon, William Cannon, Wm. Nutter.

Page 202. Clark, Richard. Will made 12 Mar 1821. Proved: 17 April 1821. Heirs: I bequeath to Leah Long and her daughter Hetty Robinson Long, the house where Mrs. Ann Powell now lives and 3 acres of cleared land around said House. Son, Elijiah Bell Clark, the house and plantation where on I live except that given Leah Long and her daughter, all the land in four pieces- "Conclusion to Lively" and "Chance" and the piece bought of Armwell Long called "Long's Discovery." Other 6 children: Sidenham Thorn, Polly, William, Betsy, Jean and Sally, all the remaining land I bought of Peter L. Berry (by Isaiah Long and myself as tenants in Common), known as "Unity Grove Enlarged" still call, also a separate parcel called "Chance" where Isaac Long lives. Ex: Henry Bell of Philadelphia Wit: Major Benson, Absolom Davis, Isaac Long. Codicil: If Ex. Henry Bell dies before Elijah Bell Clark turns 21, other 6 children to have immediate possession of their lands.

Page 205. Laws, Joshua. Will made 27 March 1821. Proved 24 April 1821. Farm I live on in Cedar Town, part of "Cedar Town Tract" to three sons, Elijah Laws, John Laws and Joshua Laws. To son Daniel, rents and profits of my farm where on my son Daniel Laws now lives and called "Farmers Delight." To the creditors of Daniel Laws and after the rest and profits of said farm shall satisfy the debts that are now due them. My will and desire is that my son Samuel Laws shall have the farm. Daughter, Ann Polk Latchum my walnut dining table. Negro girl Mary shall be manumitted and set free. Negro boy David shall be manumitted and set free at age 25. Ex: son John Laws. Wit William Burton, Sary Coverdale

Page 206. Houston, Joseph, farmer. Will made 3 April 1821. Proved: 24 April 1821 Heirs: wife Mary Houston, 1/3 part of my estate real and personal; sons, Robert and Leonard; daughters Sally and Nancy Houston and Comfort Crab. Granddaughter Mary Beach. Son Nottingham Houston, all my land as long as he pays my sons Robert and Leonard $200 each. Ex: son Nottingham Houston. Witnesses: Edward Dingle, Jr. Wm. Dunning, and Stephen Hill.

Page 208. Bonnewell, Soverign. Will made 24 January 1816. Proved: 8 May 1821. Heirs: wife Ann, the plantation during her natural life or widowhood, then to my two daughters Mary and Ann Bonnewell, if either should die then to my daughters Jane Suel and Susan Elliott. My daughter Lettica, all my money out of my Father's Benjamin Bonnewell's Estate. Ex: wife Ann Bonnewell. Wit: Josiah Polk, Sylvester Harvey, and William Vaughn.

Page 208. Marsh, Thomas, Sr. yeoman, Lewes - Rehobeth. Will made 1 April 1816. Proved: 12 May 1821. Heirs: James Marsh, plantation purchased of Captain Stone and wife, called "Warren Lot," exception of one acre. Son Thomas Marsh, Northwestern part of plantation whereon I now live, including the house. Son Jon Marsh, Southeastern part of Plantation. Daughters Mary, Jane and Nancy. Son Peter Marsh, lands purchased of William Bignal on road that leads to Lewes adjoining lands formerly John Paynter and Peter Marsh (dec'd) and lands of Dr. White, William Dodd and also the land which I purchased of Thomas Paynter who conveyed the same to my Brother Peter Marsh, who conveyed to me, land of Molly Johnson Pond, near the head waters of Kings Creek. Rents off the lands devised to Peter Marsh, exclusive of dower be applied to the schooling of my son Peter Marsh. Also to Peter Marsh, fee simple, my marsh at Kinks Bushes. To Thomas P. Marsh and John Marsh my hay marsh purchased of Alburtus Jacobs. Daughter Harriot Perry, one Eagle or $10. Daughter Catherine Thompson one acre and 1/2 of "Old Field" whereon her husband erected a small house. Ex: Wife Ann Marsh (Ref) and son Thomas P. Marsh. Wit: William Dodd, Matthew W. Marsh

Page 210. Salmons, Benjamin, farmer Will made July 1820 Proved 9 June 1821 Heirs: wife Betsy Salmons. Daughter Betsy Sammons, 150 acres of my land including house to be laid off joining up to the land that I lately sold to David Moore and on the NW side of a line drawn NE that consists of a part of three different tracts "Aydelots Fancy" "Salmons Addition" and "Eight Lotts," from a marked white oak standing at the SW edge of the St. Road that leads from Indian River to Dagsborough near the eastern most corner of Isaac Waples (heirs) land. The remaining part to Grandson Benjamin Salmon, son of Robert. The 115 acres of marsh laying on Benjamin Burton and the Wharton's Mill Pond bought of Simon Kollock to be sold. Granddaughter Annah Salmons (a Cripple), Granddaughters Drewilla Ottwel and Betsy Ottwell (Both minors), Granddaughter Lucy Salmon. Estate divided as follows, daughter 2/6's,each granddaughter 1/6. Wit: Hannah Mumford, Edward Dingle.

Page 212. Hemmons, John. Will made 29 March 1821. Proved 18 June 1821. Heirs: Daughter, Nancy Johnson sole Ex. And 1/2 the land to Grandson John Brereton Hemman the other 1/2 of the land. Son William Hemmons, 5 shillings, Heirs of my son Thomas Hemmons sum of one shilliing. Granddaughter Anna Hemmons, One cow. Wit: Sarah Griffith, Syrus Talman, Purnel Talmon, Sr.

Page 213. Johnson, Benjamin. Will made 9 March 1811. Proved .11 July 1821, heirs: Daughter Polly Smith; Son John Johnson, a tract of land 50 acres called "Bottom" also part of a tract called "Hog Island" which joins "Bottom."Daughter Rebecca Carpenter. Son Wingate Johnson 50 acres next to Schelield Rounds[?] also a tract call "Johnson Vents" containing 50 acres. Son Tilghman Johnson; Daughter Betsy Ennis; Son Annanias Johnson; Son Benjamin Johnson, my house. Daughters Nancy and Sally. Ex wife Lovey Johnson (ref) and son Annanias Johnson. Wit: Robert Robinson, Samuel Jefferson, and Loews Spicier.

Page 215. Gibbons, Josiah. Will Made 29 July 1821. Proved 21: August 1821, Heirs: 20 Acres of land bought from James Messick to be sold to raise and school my three daughters, Louise, Nancy and Jane. To son Caudwell W. Gibbons. Wit: Noah James, Elizabeth Smith, and Helen Beauchum.

Page 216. Lank, Alice, Broadkiln. Will made 21 August 1821. Proved: 28 August 1821. ½ my property to Lavinia Linch, my mother during her natural life, the other ½ to Naomi Mysee, my sister. Ex: my friend John Starr. Wit: Joseph Maull, Joshua Coverdale, and Elizabeth Starr.

Page 216 Hanzer, Thomas. Will made 15 May 1821 Proved 18 May 1821. To my wife Elizabeth 1/3 part of my lands and $1. To daughter Sara Sack(?) $1. Grandson Jesse Hanzar 25 cents, Grandson Elija Rigway $1. Grandson Cary Hanzer 25 cents. Grandson Nathaniel Hanzer 25 cents. Granddaughter Comely Hanzer 25 cents. Son Peary Hanzar 25 cents. Son John 25 cents. Son Elwande Hanzar 25 Cents. My Jacob, a certain piece of my land on the East part of the old orchard standing from the bank Line of the old Prettyman's Tract Running Parrelly with the (?) fence until comes to the north Corner of the old orchard fields, then a course that will give him his house and five acres to the Hammons Line and ¼ of a acre. The grave yard never to be sold. To him his life time and then to his eldest daughter; also the Bead that lent him and no more. I give to my son Nehemiah Hanzar, all the Remainder of my lands that I now dwell on, if he has no heirs then to my son William Hanzar. To my son William Hanzar, my daughter Jane Lobster, my daughter Ann Clark and Nehemiah Hanzar all the remaining of my moveable property. Ex: Son William Hanzar. Wit: Benjamin Richards, John Wingate.

Page 218. Hurley, Caty. Will made. 7 May 1812, Proved: 28 September 1821 Heirs: Grandson Edmund Hurley, son of John, $50 cash; four daughters Nancy Lacham, Mary Smith, Triphosa Braddy, Peggy Polk, my wearing apparel; My Negro woman Dinar to free from my heirs at my death. The rest of my personal property to be divided between my four daughter and sons Clement, Edmund and John. Ex: Two Sons Edmond Hurley and John Hurley Wit Solomon Layton, Sally Layton.

Page 219. Fisher, Samuel, Will made 27 March 1820 Proved 8-9 October 1821. To David Linch, son of Lydia Reynolds late Lydia Linch ½ part of my Estate; Daniel Fisher, son of my sister Betsy Fisher late deceased the remaining ½ part. Ex: above named Daniel Fisher(Ref) Ex given to Arthur Milby one of the creditors 9 October 1821. Wit Rebecca Breunton, Burton Robinson.

Page 219. Timmons, Aaron. Will made 19 May 1818. Proved: 4 October 1821. Youngest son Aaron, all my lands, one sorrel horse, bridle and saddle and new plow and harrow, one new grubbing hoe and new ax and five shoats, one cow yearling and bull calf and two sheep and one gun, and to take care of my wife during her life or widowhood. To my wife Comfort, one bed and furniture, one spinning wheel, one pot and cow. The residue of my person estate to be equally divided among my children Levi Timmons, Martha Littleton (wife of Abraham), Lulu Collins (wife of William Collins), Comfort Timmons, Kessiah Brittingham (wife of Solomon Britingham) and the above named Aaron. To son, John Timmons, one shilling. Ex: Son Aaron Timmons, youngest son. Wit: Isaac Cannon, Eliza Cannon

Page 220. Fleetwood, William. Will made 21 September 1820. Proved 23 March 1821. To wife Elizabeth Fleetwood, all my lands during her natural life, then to my three sons, equally divided, William Fleetwood, Sirus Fleetwood and John Fleetwood. To my wife, Elizabeth, my Negro man Eden. Moveable estate to be divided between my daughters Polly Connaway, Rebecca Jones, Eliza Fleetwood, Lovey(?) Fleetwood and Betsy Fleetwood. Ex: Wife Elizabeth Fleetwood. Wit David Hudson, Curtis Spicer, John Fleetwood.

Page 222. Mumford, John. Will Made 24 May 1821. Proved 30 October 1821. To my son, Samuel Mumford the farm and plantation on which I now live the same consisting of about 103 acres of land and hereon by the name of "Self Defiance" and in case the said Samuel should die without lawful heir the above mention farm and plantation to go to heirs two brothers, Jesse and Isaac to be equally divided. To my son Jesse Mumford, all my forest land consisting of about 77 acres, the same being a part of two tracts of land the one being called "Forest Flower" and the other "Cedar Grove," if he should die then to Samuel and Isaac. To son Isaac my river farm "Duck Head" containing 100 acres. If he should die then to Samuel and Jesse. To my daughter Hannah all my moveable property, if she should die then to my sons Samuel, Jesse and Isaac. To son William Mumford one dollar. Ex: Son Samuel Mumford. Wit: W. Dingle, Paul Waples.

Page 223. Walton, Joseph. Proved: 1 November 1821. To wife Mary, all my real and personal property. Sons Samuel, Charles and Joseph Walton to remain with their mother while single and to carry on the farm. To sons, Samuel and Charles, all my real estate to be equally divided. My daughter, Jane Hand. Son George a note I hold on him by John Bennett, Sr. To son Joseph and daughter Mary, all my personal property. Ex: Wife Mary, Daughter Mary (Ref 24 October 1821) and Son Joseph Walton. Wit Joseph Sudler, Thomas Jones, Millia Jones.

Page 225. Knowles, Robert:.Will made: 10 October 1820. Proved: 30 October 1821. My personal property to be equally divided between my three children, John, Sarah and William Knowles. My real estate to be equally divided between my two sons, John and William. Ex: John Dashial (Ref 30 October 1821). Wit: Luther Moore, Thomas T. Moore

Page 226. Parramore, Stephen. Will made 24 July 1819. Proved: 7 November 1821. To son Solomon 20 cents. To wife Unice Parramore, 1/3 of my land during her natural life provided she will keep my youngest child to arrive at age 12 and give him reasonable schooling, she may have 1/2 the profits of my land till he reaches that age and 1/3 of my moveable lands. As to my lands my will is that they be equally divided between my daughter Mary, Stephen, Lacy, Comfort, Nancy, Peter, Ebenezer, Anarotta, Tabitha and Oing(?). My Granddaughter Elizabeth Morris to have $10. Ex: son Stephen Parramore and James Pettyjohn, son of Ebenezar. Wit: Zadock James, William Maxfield, Lavinor Warring. Unica Palmore appeared 7 November 1821 and stated she would not abide by the will.

Page 227. Moore, Matthew. Will made 7 September 1818. Proved 30 November 1821. Eldest son Riston Moore, $50, Daughter, Betsy Benton $40 cash, daughter Levinia Phillips $40 Cash, daughter Louisa Moore $40 cash, Daughter Sally Moore $100, Daughter Tincey Moore $100, daughter Terazy(?) $40, daughter Lova Moore $100. The plantation whereon I now reside, the plantation where Tindal Phillips now resides, (?) the plantation where Cornelius (?) now resides and the plantation where Charles Moore, Sr. now resides and the plantation where Leonard Moore now resides and the land purchased of Tormanz Agenta Called "Jobs Lot" and "Cakers Choice." Also the land bought of James Baker, Sr. and James Baker. With all the Lands belonging to me named and not named with all my personal Estate to be equally divided between my five sons, Matthew Moore, Jr., Garrettison Moore, Warren Moore, Jonathan Moore and Benjamin Moore. Ex: Wife Ester Moore. Wit: Elzey Moore, Charles Moore, and Leonard Moore.

Page 229. Holland Albert. Will made: 10 March 10(?)2 - Proved. 11 December 1821. All my estate to my brother John William. Ex: John Holland. Wit: John White, William Jacobs. Phillips Kollock appeared and stated that said William departed this life some time ago. 1 December 1821

Page 229. Wingate, Ann. Will Made 25 June 1818. Proved 19 December 1821. Heirs: John Wingate - Land. Son Mitchel Wingate land called "Last Chance." Son Thomas Wingate, Son Ephram Wingate. Granddaughter Sally Elgate, daughter of Hershiah(?)Wingate, daughter Lavinia Jones, Son Joshua Wingate, Son Phillip Wingate, son Joshua Wingate. Ex: Joshua Wingate. Wit: James Webb, Elizabeth Thompson, widow, Comfort B. Webb. *Note: this is a difficult will to read d as it is all written in a backhand handwriting*

Page 231, Spicer, Betsy, Broad Creek Hundred. Will Made: 7 January 182(?). Proved: 15 January 1822. To my granddaughter, Julia Ann Dickinson, one bed and furniture, and one cow and calf. Granddaughter, Myranda Short, one bed and furniture. The rest of my estate to be equally divided between my sons, Shaderick Short, Edward Short, Phillip Short and Isaac Short and my daughters Sally Marvil, Polly Redden and Betsy Dickinson. Ex: Son Phillip Short. Wit: David Hudson, Eleanor Short.

Page 232. Prettyman, William. Will made: 12 May 1818. Proved: 15 January 1822. To daughter Peggy Prettyman, the land bought off Levin Milby and the land where she now lives until my grandson Zadock Milby comes to age 21. And the 1/3 of said land during her natural life and I give the said lands to be equally divided between the five children of Levin Milby (dec'd) Zadock Milby, Nathaniel Milby, Ann T. Milby, William P. Milby and Benjamin I. Milby. That is to say 2/3 of said lands when Grandson Zadock Milby comes of age and the other 1/3 after the decease of my daughter Peggy. To Peggy Prettyman, a bond I have on Cannon Prettyman for $137, she is to pay ½ of said bond to my daughter Betty Derickson, wife of Ephraim Derickson. To Patty Evans, my housekeeper, one bed and furniture and walnut dressing table. To my son James Prettyman the land on which I now live. If James should die without issue that the lands to descend to my Grandson William Prettyman Milby. Then, also, if James dies without issue ½ my personal estate to descend to the children of Peggy Cannon Prettyman and the other half to the children of Betty Derickson. Ex: Brother Benjamin Prettyman, Wit: Comfort Prettyman, Hetty Prettyman.

Page 233. Ingram, Joshua. Will made: 11 January 1822- Proved 15 January 1822. To my son Job Ingram ten dollars, To son John Ingram all my land being on the Northwest side of my Mill Pond and all my little tract on the said sides of said branch adjoining thereto, also ¼ of the lands bought of Benton Harris generally called by me the "Robinson Place;" also one yoke of oxen, one bed and furniture, To my daughter Sally Ingram, that I had by Nancy Thomas, all my land and marsh on the Island and also the piece of land bought of Drake Miller, my best desk, one silver tea pot, one silver Mil(?), one bed and furniture , one large looking glass and $200. To my sons, I had with Nancy Thomas, named Samuel Ingram, Nathaniel Ingram and Joshua Ingram all my lands not already

49

willed. All my moveable property to be divided between my children John
Ingram, Samuel Ingram, Nathaniel Ingram, Joshua Ingram and Sally Ingram.
Ex: Son John Ingram. Wit: James Webb, George Messick, and Sarah
Stephenson.

Page 234. Houston, Robert. Will made 4 November 1821. Proved 15 January
1822. To son John T. Houston, a Tract of land call "P(?) Ridge" and other
lands paying Ann Laws Houston $100. To Isaac Howard Houston the "Green
Swamp Tract" lying next to his brother Robert, which is next to the land of
Wm. Burton's Heirs, at head of Indian River. Road toward "Brookfield,"
which some call the "Wolf Pit Road," he paying my daughter Elizabeth M.
Short $100. To son Joseph Aydelott Houston, land, marshes and pasture
which adjoins the above he paying $100 to Sally Burton Houston. To Robert
Bell Houston, my home place, his mother to enjoy the use until he reaches
age 21. To daughter Elizabeth Short $300. Daughter Arm Laws Houston
$300. Daughter Sally Burton Houston $300. The rent of John Houston's
lands to be put to the use of schooling Robert, Joseph and Sally Houston. Ex:
Wife Ann Houston and John Thoroughgood. Wit: Phillip Wingate and
George Messick.

Page 236. Wilson, John. Will made: 19 December 1822 - Proved: 28 January 1822.
Son Joseph Wilson, all the lands that lays between my two mill branches to the
southward of a line drawn from a marked (?) standing near the tail of my Saw Mill,
south 55 ½ degrees through my land until it intersects the second line of a piece of
land laid off at the west end of a little mill dam and no more. To my wife, all my land
that lay to the east side of my Mill Pond and between the said pond and branch and
- roads that leads from Thomas Johnson's to the - where Sarah Gibbons formerly
lived and adjoining the lands of Mannan Bull, Joseph Copes and Thomas Johnson, at
her death to become the property of son John Wilson. To son John Wilson the one
half part of my Saw Mill and Grist Mill where I now live with one half of the (?) plank
and stock yard, To Son Daniel Wilson the two following Tracts, "Poplar Ridge" and
"Wilson's Folly" by lands of Peter Fletch, Edmund Fletcher, Short's heirs and James
Gumby, during his natural life then to my Grandson ,John Wilson, son of Daniel
Wilson. To son William Wilson, Tract of land known as "Johnson Chance" formerly
belonging to Isaiah Johnson, bounded by land of Cannon's heirs and Joseph Wilson.
To son Benjamin Wilson, Tract of land "Third Choice" where I formerly lived, part of
"Safety" and part of "Gibraltar and part of "Condition" To Hickory Ridge adjoining
"Third Choice." To son Stephen Wilson and part of "Third Choice" and a part of
"Gibraltar" bounded by the land of John Truitt and Thomas Truitt and Phillips Heirs
during his natural life then to become the property of my Granddaughter Sally
Wilson, daughter of Stephen Wilson. To my Daughter Hannah Betts, where she now
lives and it fell to me by my Father's decease during her natural life then to my
Grandson John Betts, if he dies without lawful issue then to my son Benjamin
Wilson. To Grandson John Truitt, son of John Truitt of Jas. To my

Daughter Prissilla Hill. The remainder of my estate to my four children John Wilson, William Wilson, Benj. Wilson, Holland Truitt, wife of John Truitt. Ex: Son John Wilson and William Wilson. Wit: Samuel Gibbons, ??ecah Truitt

Page 238. Williams, Samuel, planter. Proved: 15 February 1822. To my Daughter-in-law Allison Williams during her widowhood all the lands that was devised to me by Isaac Train, Esq. at her death to James Williams and Luther Martindale Williams, provided the Allison/Allisfare pays to my son Elijah Williams the sum of $80. To son Elijiah Williams fifty acres of land called "Parmers Folly," also a Tract called "Joshua Lott." Ex: Elijiah Williams. Wit: Samuel Elliott, Elijah Melson, and Polly Melson.

Page 240. Burton, Sophia, widow, Long Neck, Indian River. Will Made: 4 January 1822. Proved: 12 February 1822. To granddaughter Margaret N. Ingram, Daughter of Jobe Ingram, one cherry tree Chest. To Son John Burton, all the remainder of my estate, real and personal. Ex: John Burton. Wit: James T. Baylis, James F. Baylis.

Page 241. Griffith, John. Will made. 6 January 1822. Proved 21 July 1822. To my four sons, Bolitha Griffith, Seth Griffith, Turner Griffith and James Griffith all my lands and Tenements to be equally divided. Daughter Nancy Coverdale, two cows and 2 yearlings. Daughter Polly Austan, one cow. Daughter Eliza Coats, one heifer. Son Joshua Griffith, one shilling. Son William Griffith, one Shilling. Son John Griffith, one Shilling. Wife Christianna and my four sons all the remainder of my estate to be equally divided Ex: Wife Christianna and Son Bolitha Griffith, Wit: Samuel Stephens, Isaac Coverdale, James B. Raston.

Page 241. Morris, Bevens. Will made 23 March 1819. Proved: 27 February 1822. Wife Sarah Morris one horse, one share, all my house furniture except to beds To my wife, all the tract of land, 100 bushels of corn, 10 bushels of wheat, one ox cart, two plows, two harrows, Two (?) chains, four cows and calves, two hoes, two spades, six heads of sheep and all the wool now in the house and all the flax in the Shaw, all the geese and poultry, ten head of hogs and one sow and pigs together with the thirds of all the lands and marshes down the neck where William Conwell and Abram Conwell formerly lived during her natural live and no more. To son John Morris, 100 bushels of corn and one ox cart at Phillip Heveloes Negro. Son William Morris, one black mare, bridle and saddle and yoke of steers lately broken, one cow and calf and one gun I bought of William Steel, one bed and furniture. Son Robert Morris, one yoke of young bundle steers, one cow and calf and one new small gun. To my sons, John, William and Robert all my lands and marshes down the neck where Abraham and William Conwell formerly lived except for one acre of Sedar (?) with the Rails now split on said swamp and all the lands where Phillip Hevelow Negro now lives from the Beaverdam Branch To Groves Road, adj. Lands of Simpson Hazzard, John Hazzard and Samuel Cade also 80 acres of fresh marsh on south side of Prime Hook Creek adj. a lot or bank where Absolom M. Conely lives and 8 acres running to C(?) Landing, to be equally divided. If either John or William or Robert Morris dies without lawful issue the land to be divided between surviving brothers. If more than one dies without issue to be equally divided among my three daughters Elizabeth Lofland, Sarah Wiltbank and Amelia Morris. To granddaughters Mary and Eliza Morris all the lands and marsh lying on the north side of Groves Road down to Prime Hook Creek except the two lots of marsh before mentioned. If one of my granddaughters die her portion to be divided between Elizabeth Lofland and Sarah Wiltbank. If both die then to be divided between my three daughters. To Elizabeth Lofland $600. To Sarah Wiltbank $600. To Amelia Morris $1000 in fourths to be paid at age 18 the remainder at age 21. The remainder of moveable property, except for Legacies to sons, equally divided. Wearing apparel, to sons William and Robert Morris. To son William my silver watch. Ex: Son John Morris. Wit: John Conwell, Jeremiah Conwell.

Page 243. Truitt, Elizabeth. Will made: 7 June 1820. Proved: 4 March 1822. Daughter Amelia Truitt, all my Estate both Real and personal consisting of a piece of land I bought of my daughter Nancy Truitt containing 16 acres, also eight head of cattle, also seven head of hogs also with a (?) of household goods. Ex: Daughter Amelia Truitt Wit: Isaac Ingram, John Ingram, Henry Hudson.

Page 244. Tindal, Minos. Will made 22 January 1822 - Proved: 25 March 1822. My land be divided between my sons Leden and Miles Tindal by a line beginning at my Saw Mill and thence with the road through my land as it now stands till it intersects the line between my lands and Purnell Tindal's lands. The land on the South of said road to be Leden's part and that on the West Side where my buildings stand to Miles. If either should die without issue then the whole to the other, by paying each of my daughters $50. Until my son arrives at 21. Son Samuel. That my ½ of the sawmill and Grist mill and ½ the ? and plank yards be sold. My sons Miles and Leden to keep my son Samuel Tindal, if he should marry then to pay him $100 each. Ex: Brother Purnel Tindal. Wit: Miles Tindal, Nancy Tindal and William Bell.

Page 243. Gunby, Stephen Will Made 6 April 1822. Proved: 23 April 1822. To wife Neomy Gunby, 1/3 part of real and personal estate during natural life and widowhood. Son David Gunby, ½ of all my lands. Son Jacob Gunby the other ½ part of my lands. Daughter Arroney Gunby $80 to be paid by Jehu? Short for which he is due me for his raising and also $68 to be paid Sally Betts late Sally Short for her raising. To Zipporaugh Short, 1 shilling. To Elizabeth (Urner?) 1

Shilling. The remainder of my estate to be divided between my 5 children. Ex: Neomy Gunby, wife and David Gunby, son. Wit: James Betts, Isaac Short.

Page 245. Copes, Joseph. Will made: 27 March 1822 Proved: 23 April 1822. To my wife Letty, the farm and plantation whereon Job Lawles now resided that she may go immediately into possession after my decease, as soon as the Tenant can move. The said lands to be divided in the following manner: Beginning at a marked pine Sapling in a dry ditch near the north corner of the field on the west side of the Road, Thence North 65 degrees west ninety four perches to a corner Oak in the line of the land now in possession of Rev. Caudwell Windsor. Thence, Beginning again at said pine sapling and running along said ditch south 19 degrees, west thirty and a half perches to a corner Locust tree by the road, and one perch further into said road, and thence along the same south forty seven degrees, west eighteen perches to a wet ditch; thence up and the same South sixty nine degrees, East fourteen perches, South eighty and a half, East twelve perches East and one hundred perches North, sixty three perches East, Eleven and a half perches to a small marked maple by a bridge; thence South twelve and a half degree east twenty perches to a post by a fence thence along the same south thirty one degrees West twenty-eight perches, thence south sixty perches,ending near the line of James Collins land. Thence South eighty one degrees, West one hundred and seventy perches to an old road leading near Bridget's house, thence along the said road and the line of Culdwell Windsor's land, to the corner Red Oak first mentioned, containing one hundred fifty seven acres, ninety of which are now in Orchards and cultivation and the remainder wood land. To belong to my said wife during her natural life and then to descend to my daughter Hester. I also give to said wife the still, best horse and carriage, Magh. Chest, one bed and furniture, cow and calf and 6 chairs. However, if my wife decides to have her dower by Law then the foregoing provisions shall be void, in that case, I give my daughter Hester $59. one bed and furniture and no more. Should Hester die before her Mother and without heir, the said lands to belong to my older children. After the dower of my wife the remainder of my lands to be divided by order of Orphan's Court. Dividing the intestate lands of my late wife Jane, formerly Jane W. White, that the whole be divided among her children, To my children Isaac, Betsy, Thomas, Mary, Leah, Nancy, Jane, James and Joseph. Ex: my son Isaac and my wife. Wit: Elizabeth White, James Vessels, James N. Perry. On 18 April 1822, Letty Copes agrees to terms of the will. Wit: James Vessels, Paynter Waples. Mary H. Copes. *Note: Plat Map included with Will.*

Page 248. Burton, Daniel. (Lewes-Rehobeth Hundred). Will made: 7 April 1822 Proved 9 May 1822. To wife Polly Shepherd Burton, the dwelling house in which I now live, together with five acres including the out houses, except the smith's shop adjoining the creek or tail way or branch and the County Road next to the Mill. Also to wife my interest in the Mill which I hold with the heirs of

Daniel Burton, which I devised by the death of my father Woolsey Burton, being one half thereof the whole of the above mentioned property to her lands during her natural life. At her death to my surviving children. To son Benjamin my silver watch, my largest gun and $50. And 1/5 part of share of my estate, To son John Hilliard, $100. To be applied to his schooling and 1/5 part of my estate. To my two sons, Daniel and David, $200 each to be applied to their schooling and 1/5 part each of my estate. To son Peter Robinson, $200 to be applied to his schooling and 1/5 part of my estate. The executor to have the Orphan's Court to divide the land for my children and hold in trust until they come of age. Ex: and guardians: Brothers, Benjamin and Meirs Burton. Wit Elizabeth Lyons, Jehu Stockley, Levi Hill.

Page 250. Collins, Joseph. Will Made: 10 April 1822. Proved: 15 May 1822. To son Ephraim one Shilling, To son William, one Shilling, To James A Collins, Noah R. Collins and Mary R. Collins, the three children of my son Joseph Collins one shilling each. To my son John Collins $100, also one gray horse, one feather bed and furniture and one black cow. To my daughter, Elenor Knowles, one shilling. To my son Thomas all my lands called "Moores Privilege Enlarged." The remainder of my estate to my two sons, John Collins and Thomas Collins. Ex: Son Thomas Collins. Wit: William Elzy, Levi Collins, Benjamin Collins.

Page 251. Holland, John. Will written: 25 October 1821. Proved: 15 May 1822. Wife Elizabeth Holland, ½ of the lands purchased from William Mathist, where I now live and ½ the lands purchased from Samuel Johnson. And ½ of all the (?) I now own, and ½ of the land I purchased of Robinson Manlove, during her widowhood and for her to school and raise my two youngest children with the same, and if she should marry then to have only 1/3 of the afsd. land and marsh. Also to my wife, my young bay horse, bed and furniture and 8 head of cattle of her choice, ten head of hogs, all my plows and harrows, axes, hoes and all my geese and poultry, and if she does not stand to my will then for her to have $50 of my estate. To son Elisha Holland all the land and parcels in the State of Maryland in Worcester County, if he should die without heir, land to be divided among the rest of my children. To my daughter Mary Hazzard, one cow and calf one yoak of oxen and all the Negroes that she has had and all the goods she has had, not to come into the appraisement of my estate. To son John Holland, all the lands purchased of Robert Neill and all the land purchased of Elias Baker and part of the lands purchased of John Neill as follows: beginning at the Lerales(?) line and at the county road and running the road that leads from Milton to Coolspring, till it intersects Perry's line, leaving the Road to the division line between my two sons, John and Joseph Holland. To Joseph Holland, the remaining part of the lands purchased of John Neill and all the land I purchased of James Speeais and 90 acres of land purchased of William Martin and wife. To son James all the profits from the lands I purchased of Robinson Manlove and from the lands purchased of Samuel Johnson and all the profits of all the marsh I own on that side of the gut leading from Broadkiln Creek. To a glade between Charles King, and me except the marsh I purchased of Stephen Coston and Thomas Russell. To son Ebenezar Holland, all the lands purchased of William Mathias and all the marsh their belonging where I now live and fifteen acres of marsh if purchased of Stephen Coston, the marsh purchased of Thomas Russell and all the land purchased of Jacob Hazzard. Also Negro boy named Phillip. To daughter Magdalin Holland, one bed and furniture and Negro girl named Jane, two cows and calves and $300 in cash when she arrives at age 21. If she should die without heir to my youngest daughter Tabitha. To Tabitha Holland one bed and furniture, two cows and calves, one Negro boy named Elzey and $300. To Grandson Elisha Holland (Under 21) $5. To grandson John Holland (Under 21) $50. Grandson William Holland (Under 21) $50. To Granddaughter Tabbitha Holland (Under 21) $50. Ex: wife Elizabeth Holland. Wit: John Starr, Barak Richards, and Elizabeth Starr.

Page 253. Townsend, Littleton. Will made: 9 September 1820. Proved: 21 May. 1821. Wife Betsy, all the lands wherein I now live and at the decease to son William. To sons John, James, Major and William and daughter Sarah Dazey, equal and full partnership in hay marsh at the bottom of Cedar Neck, part of a tract called "Addition" about 20 acres each. To Grandson James Townsend Dazey, son of Amos Dazey and my daughter Sarah, 31 acres called "Townsends Discovery" where Amos and Sarah now live. To my son William, my gray mare, one cow and calf, one sow and pigs, and all the farming utensils. To my Grandson, Littleton, my compass, chain scale and dividers. To Grandson Peter all my Arithmetic Books. To the rest of my Grandchildren, not mentioned before, one dollar each. Ex: Son John Townsend. Wit: Jacob A, Clark, and Rhoda Clark

Page 255. Bloxam, Richard. Will made: 2 September 1806. Proved: 21 May 1822. To daughter Nancy, wife of John Dorman, my house and grounds at the head of Broadkiln, where she now lives, and 20 feet of land front, from Woolsy Hall's to the public ground, also 40 ft front at the creek, the Lewes side of the cripple to build a wharf, his granary and the one already built to make a passage to — creek. Also, to have 15 pounds and #20. To daughter Frances a lot of ground adjoining Nancy Dorman's lot 35 feet front from street to street. To daughter Hester (U21), a lot of ground 30 feet front from street to street and 30 pounds. Daughter Alice (U21) ground adjoining Hester's, 30 feet front from Street to street. To sons Robert and John my wharf and granary at the head of Broadkiln, also my land and plantation, whereon I now live to be equally divided. To my daughters Alice and Hester 30 feet each front on wharf lot to build each of them a house or granary on. To my daughter Margaret 30 or 40 feet front from the street on the Creek to build a wharf. To my seven children the old field I own at the head of Broadkiln on Federal Street and Walnut Street to be equally divided. To my sons, Robert and John, the residue of my estate. Ex: son Robert and daughter Margaret. Wit: Joshua Glover and Samuel Paynter, Jr.

Page 256. Donovan, Foster. Will made: 8 October 1821. Proved: 27 May 1822. To wife, Priscilla Donovan, one horse, one cow and calf, 2 feather beds and furniture and one corner cubbard. To my son Eli, $25. To son Reuben Donovan, the farm where he now lives, I purchased of Avery Conwell, over the division line running as follows: at a Stake on the line of James Redden, thence S 75 degrees, East 60 perches. Thence, North 65, East 28 perches. To the Vine border of Troublesome Ridge, thence North 24 degrees, east perches, Thence North 65 degrees, East 26 perches, Thence South 77 degrees East 24 perches to a White Oak standing by road to Melan, Thence with S Road, south 85 degrees, east 28 perches, thence on south 82 degrees, east 11 perches to a White Gum at the intersection of the County road that Cade to Milton and unto Ruben Donovan. To son, Gorge Donovan, all the cleared land and woodland that lies on E. side of a division line between Sons Donovan and Burton Donovan. To Luke Donovan, all the farm where he now lives. To son Burton, my home farm. Daughter Nebany Carpenter 5 shillings. Daughter Priscilla $5. Rest of estate to wife. Ex: wife Priscilla Donovan. Wit: James Redden, Robert Collins, Jesse Dutton.

Page 258. Rouse, James, Broadkiln. Will made: 8 May 1820. Proved 4 June 1822. Wife Henrietta Rouse (Ex), my entire real and personal property during her widowhood. After the marriage or death of my wife Henrietta, the said property to Mary Ann Fowler. Wit: Peter S. Parker, Joseph Maull.

Page 259. Hasting, Daniel. Will made: 11 July 1822. Proved 16 July 1822. To son Michael, all the lands I purchased of the Heirs of John Nelms, and lands bought of Phillip Collins, lands bought of Josiah Collins, a small piece bought of Elenander Collins, a piece bought of Joshua Culver, being near land of Thomas Hearn, a piece bought of Henry Hasting, which was taken up and surveyed by and for Wm. Elzey. To Levi Hasting, my home plantation including land bought of Melvin Hasting. To son, Benjamin, the remainder of the lands. Remaining part of my estate to be divided among all my children: Michael Hasting, Lydia (wife of Elihu), Levi Hastin, Benjamin Hastin, Relli[sic] Hasting, Henry Hasting and Winney Hasting. Ex: Son in Law, Elihu Hasting. Wit: William Elzey, Hesekiah Hasting.

Page 260. Fleetwood, Whittingham, Nanticoke Hundred. Will made: 4 February 1822. Proved: 30 July 1822. To cousin, William Fleetwood, all my share of my

Mother's estate now in the hands of John and Nehemiah Fleetwood. To the above named William Fleetwood $10.34 which Peter Robinson, Esq. is now due me. To cousin, Syrus Fleetwood, all that is due me from the estate of William Fleetwood, dec'd. also the sum of $31.18 due me from Wm. Brady of New Castle and Appoquinimink Hundred in the State of Delaware, $10 due me from Hugh Walls, also a gun at the house of Benjamin Walls in New Castle County. Ex: Aunty Betty Fleetwood (Ref- 30 July 1822) Wit: Daniel Hudson, William Jones.

Page 261. Lockwood, Benjamin. Will made 20 April 1809 Proved: 5 August 1822. Item my black man Cato to be free. To John Lockwood Christopher, son of my granddaughter Elizabeth Christopher $30. 1/7 part of my estate to Nancy Gray, Hannah Christopher, Sally Hickman, William Christopher, Isaac Christopher, and Rebecca Tracy (Children of my daughter Elizabeth Jacobs). 1/7 part to Rebecca Aydelotte, Betsey Howard, Sarah Johnson, Archdah Aydelotte, Mary Aydelotte, Benjamin Lockwood, Nancy Lockwood and Lydia Lockwood (children of my son Wm.). 1/7 part to my daughter Mary Salmons. 1/7 part to Pheobe Lockwood, William Dingle, Edward Dingle, Jr., Anna Wingate, Betsy Dingle, Sally Wingate, Hannah Dingle and John Dingle (Children of my daughter Hannah Dingle). 1/7 part to John Hickman, Polly Houston, Nathaniel Hickman and Nancy Jacobs (children of my daughter Sally Hickman). 1/7 part to my granddaughter Elizabeth Christopher, daughter of my daughter Elizabeth Jacobs. 1/7 part to Shephard Prettyman, Nathaniel Prettyman, Perry Prettyman, Sally Prettyman, Phoebe Prettyman, Joseph Prettyman (children of my daughter Rebecca Prettyman). To my Grandson, Benjamin Lockwood, son of my son, William Lockwood, my land. Ex: Edward Dingle, Jr. Wit: Armwell Long, Joshua Robinson, and Mary Robinson. Codicil: 13 May 1816, names great-grandson John Lockwood. Wit: John Mitchell, Ewd Dingle.

Page 264 Ellegood, Thomas. Will made 9 January 1817. Proved 13 August 1822. To son John Ellegood, fifty acres of land on the south end of my land adjoining lands of John Huffington, Sr. and Manan Bull. Land where John Love (dec'd.) lived; now belonging to Jacob Morgan. To my son William, all the remaining part of my lands and dwelling house. Daughter Nancy Ellegood, one cow and calf. Daughter Betsy Ellegood, one feather bed and furniture. Remainder to four children, Polly Carey, George N. Ellegood, Nancy Ellegood and Betsey Ellegood. Also, to William a yoak of oxen. Ex: Son John Ellegood. Wit: William Ellegood, Lovey Spicer, and Peggy Knowles. Note: on 13 August 1822 Polly Ellegood is known as Peggy Adams.

Page 266. Carey, Charles. Will made: 27 March 1812. Proved 23 September 1822. To my wife's daughter Nancy Chandler, one bed, two sheets and 2 quilts.

To wife, Levina Carey, all the remainder of my estate. Ex: Lavina Carey. Wit Benjamin Henderson, Isaac Walton, and Priscilla Walton.

Page 266. Sharp, John, Nanticoke Hundred. Will Made: 13 November 1822. Proved 20 November 1822. To son Clement Sharp, land on West Side of Mire Branch. To son Elisha Sharp part of "Parsley Liking" and all of "Silver Plain," Son Job Sharp, all the land on the East of Elisha Sharp's 200 acres. Son Thomas Sharp, a tract of land adjoining lands of Burton Prettyman and Clement Sharp. To son John Sharp, a tract purchased of Selby Sharp, adjoining other lands of Selby Sharp and John Carlisle, formerly belonging to Samuel Radcliff 230 acres, To son Peter Sharp, home farm with all the lands in Nanticoke Hundred. My wife Nancy Sharp and my 5 youngest children, Elizabeth, Emeline, Rachel, John and Peter should remain on the home farm above-mentioned. To sons John Sharp (under 21) $325, Phillip Sharp (under 21) $325. I give to my three daughters Elizabeth, Emaline and Rachel 170 acres of land in Broadkiln, adjoining Robert Collins and (?) Dickinson, to be equally divided. And to my three daughters $150 each, To wife Nancy Sharp, my best horse and carriage, one cow and calf, one bed and furniture and $25. To Clement $50. Sons Job and Elisha Sharp $50 each. The rest of my estate shall be equally divided between my wife and children after paying Peggy and Nancy Tatmen $5 each. Betsy Gray, wife of William Gray $10. To William Tatman, my stepson, 2 two year old steers. Ex: Wife Nancy Sharp and sons Clement, Job and Elisha Sharp. Wit: Samuel Radcliff, Truston R. McCalley.

Page 269. Ross, Nathaniel. Will made: 17 August 1820. Proved: 30 November 1822. Wife Sally Ross, 1/3 part of my estate, if she remarries $150 per annum for her natural life if she does not stand by the will she gets nothing. Son, Curtis Ross, shall pay to my other children $500 equally divided, Property given to Curtis Ross, by his Grandfather, in Seaford, not to be appraised in estate. Ex: Wife Sally Ross and son Curtis Ross. Wit Hester Cannon, Sally Smith, Caleb Ross.

Page 270. Webb, John, Dagsborough Hundred. Will made: 7 December 1822. Proved 5 December 1822. Son John Neblet Webb, one mare colt, one gun, tanners tools, all tools in shop, use of shop for 5 years. Son, John James Webb, all my land, with use of shop, one gun, yoak of oxen (now on hire of Mr.Obed Otwell) Family Bible. Daughter Lovey Newbold Ellingsworth, one bureau, one red chest, one looking glass, 3 rush bottom chairs, Daughter, Comfort Banks Webb, one wooden Clock, one blue pine chest, one walnut breakfast table, one looking glass, arm chairs, 3 rush chairs, $20. To Nelly Thoroughgood (wife of Miller) one large chest that belonged to her father. Ex: Robert L. Harris, son-in-law, Benjamin Ellingsworth (refused). Wit: James A. Thompson, George Messick, Nelly Messick.

Page 273. Rickards, Thomas. Will made: 28 March 1821. Proved: 10 December 1822. Wife Kerin Rickards — all I possess during her natural life and widowhood. If she marries, then 1/3. At her death all my personal and real estate, equally divided between daughters Betsy and Emily. Ex: Wife Kerin Rickard. Wit: Stephen R. Lofland, Rachel Lofland, Alsy Webb.

Page 274, Perry, Margaret, of Sussex Co., but now of Philadelphia, Pennsylvania. Will made: 18 June 1822. Proved 2 January 1823. My wearing apparel to niece Nancy Marsh, also looking glass, with an eagle on top, my silver teaspoons marked with "P." Her mother is to have whatever wearing apparel she wishes. To niece Jane Wilson $20. The remainder of my estate to my nephews, Simon, Samuel, Matthew and James P. Wilson. Wit: Deborah Richards, James P. Wilson. NOTE: Rev. James P. Wilson is living at No 24 Aamron St., Philadelphia 6 January 1823.

Page 276. Walton, Polly. (Widow). Will made: 8 December 1822. Proved 7 January 1823. To son Joseph Walton, Ex. And Land containing 80 acres, lying on Herring Branch. Wit: William Pierce, Donovan Spencer, Ann May.

Page 277. Bredel, Elihu. Will Made: 29 November 1822. Proved: 18 January 1823. Son Isaac Bredel, all the lands I possess: lst in Delaware in Cedar Neck one at the Bar Trap, one at the Beaverdam. In Maryland, the beach marsh. Three daughters: Sophia Holland, Hannah Waples and Rachel Tingle all the balance of my property. Ex: Son in Law, Nathaniel Tingle. Wit: Samuel Cade, John Hall, William L. Hall

Page 277. Hazzard, Jane. Will Made: 17 July 1822. Proved 11 February 1823. To my father Jacob Richards and my Mother Elizabeth, all the lands I possess in Broadkiln Hundred. At their death, to their son Theodore W. Richards. Ex: father Jacob Richards. Wit: Peter Hall, Charles Fisher

Page 278. Collins, John. Will made: 26 January 1823. Proved: 21 July 1823. To son Thomas, one gun. Younger son, one bed and furniture. Daughter Mary Ann one bed and furniture. Eldest son William, blue chest. Rebecca Ciggress(?) Spinning wheel and red chest. I leave my tract of land 75 Acres, to be sold, the money left over after paying my debts, to my 4 children, William, Thomas, John and Mary Ann. Ex: Cozen Isaac Collins. Wit Stephen Hill, Ismy Taylor

Page 279 Willson, Sarah. Will Made: 3 January 1823. Proved 3 March 1823. To my daughter, Sarah Collins, wife of Solomon, one gray horse. Daughter Margaret Walker wife of John Walker, one cloak and wrapper which was her sister Betsey's. Daughter, Nancy Wilson, one cow, and one walnut desk, one bed and furniture, the rest to be equally divided between Sarah Collins, wife of Solomon, and Nancy Wilson. Wit: Reece Phillips, Robert Hurley.

Page 280. Heavelo, Jonathan of Broadkiln Hundred. Will made: 31 January 1821. Proved 4 March 1823. To my niece Susan, wife of John S. Conwell, $100.00 to three children of John S. Conwell, (John, Elias, Elizabeth), at the death of my sister Susan Morris Two nephews, William R. and Heavelo Morris, sons of my sister Susan Morris All the rest and residue of my estate. Sister Susan Morris to have full use of estate except $100 left to Susan Conwell. Ex: Sister Susan Morris. Wit: Thomas Draper, Samuel Paynter.

Page 282. Prettyman, John. Will made: 4 March 1823. Proved: 11 March 1823. Wife Ann Prettyman, all my land on the West side of the County Road leading from Bridgeville to Seaford call "Margaret's Venture," and all personal property during widowhood- if she marries she shall retain her third. The other 2/3 divided among my youngest children: Levin M., James H., Ann, Jacob W., Sara, John C. and Charlotte. My daughter Mary, wife of Zachariah Hatfield, and Daughter Eliza, wife of William Brown, shall have no part of my estate. That Moses Corden that married my daughter Matilda or his son, Elbert shall not have any part of my estate. Wit: William A. Polk, Tilghman Meloney, and Robert Collins.

Page 283. Baker, Isaac. Will made: 7 January 1823. Proved 13 March 1823. Wife Nancy Baker, all my real and personal estate to raise and school my children. Ex: Wife. Wit: Wooten Loyd, Mary Benson, Warren Jefferson

Page 284. West, Kendal. Will made: 17 November 1822. Proved: 25 March 1823. Heirs: Wife Esther. Daughter Mary Morris West, wife of Ebe West, the house and land to the lines of Betts and Bounds, as it was held -?- Owens before I bought it, where Henry Miller (Negro) now lives. Son Nathaniel, the house and land I dwell on, including Mill Seat. Daughter Martha Miller West, the lands where Robert Derickson now lives in White's Neck. To Henry Clayton Cottingham, $25, if wife stands to my will, if not, then no part. Ex: Son in Law, Ebe West. Wit: Major Benson, Sydinhard Clarke.

Page 285. Thompson, Littleton. Will made: 9 March 1823. Proved:29 March 1823. Wife Levina Tompson, my manor plantation where I now live. William Wesley Tompson all my lands after they are released by Levinia, whereon I now live. Daughter, Eliza Cooper Tomson. Rest divided between Sarah Hannon and Elizas Tompson. Ex: Wife Lavinia Tomson. Wit: Sarah Polk, William Wooten

Page 287. Warrington, Stephen (Broadkiln). Will made: 4 April 1823. Proved: 21 April 1823. Wife Ann, the 2 story end of the house where I now live and three acres of land. Daughter Elizabeth Stephenson, $100, for the use of her children. Daughter Arcada, $100, for the use of her children. Son Thomas, lands purchased of David Hazzard, Esq., formerly the property of William Conwell. Son Samuel Rowland Warrington, $100. Two youngest daughters, Mary and Eliza. Five elder children, Elizabeth, John, Arcada, Thomas and Samuel. Ex: Samuel Paynter, Samuel R. Paynter. Both refused. Wit: Winlock Clark, William Gorden.

Page 287. Sarnel, Sarah. Will made: 27 July 1822. Proved: 10 May 1823. Heirs:- Son John, 5 shillings, Grandson John W. Campbell, $15.00 when 21. Friend Woolsey Carry, my land, then to my Grandson John W. Campbell. Ex: Woolsey Carry. Wit: Robert Hunter, Joseph Carry.

Page 289. Smith John, (of Philadelphia). Will made: 21 October 1812, Proved 15 May 1823. Wife Rhoda, 1/3 part of rents and profits of my land, 1/5 part of moveable property. Son John D. Smith, land called ""Farmer's Delight," 1/2 land bought of Wilm. Hambleton called "Little Neck and Jack's Marsh," paying his brother Robert Jones Smith $200. Son Josiah H. Smith, 115 acres, which was devised to my Brother Henry Smith, which was called "Farmer's Delight""with 1/2 of "Little Neck Marsh." To my daughter Mary C. Smith, Eliza Smith, Robert James Smith, all the lands and Mills on Prime Hook Creek, in the County of Sussex, State of Delaware, formerly called "Curwithing Mills and Land," bought. of John Davis, Thomas and Samuel Collins with 100 acres of marsh in Prime Hook, Deed from Luke Walton and Henry Smith (Dec'd) with 10 shares in Farmers and Merchants Bank to be equally divided. Wit: Bolitha Glass, Joseph Ray. States that Samuel Paynter, Esq. is age 54, and Daniel Godwin is age 49. They attesting to signatures of Bolitha Glass and Joseph Ray.

Page 290. Figgs, Emilia. Proved: 5 June 1823. To Cyrus C. Windsor, the balance of my money left, 1 chest and one trunk. To Shadrack Hall's daughters, Eleanor and Maria, one dress and one pair of stockings apiece. The balance of my clothes and property to Nancy Windsor and her daughter Nancy (or Jancy). Wit: Major Lewis, George Benson.

Page 290. Burton, Samuel. Will made: 22 April 1823. Proved: 17 June 1823. Wife Elizabeth, $150 to be levied out of my estate on condition that she builds her a house on my plantation called "Kinnings"; but if she chooses not to do so, wife shall receive $50 and 1/3 part of Estate. To my children Elizabeth Craige Burton and Samuel Alfred Burton, the whole of 2/3 of the lands for 13 years, after 13 years to be equally divided among my three sons namely Henry Burton, David Early Burton and Samuel Alfred Burton. Remainder to be divided between all my children: Patience Burton, Henry Burton, Louisa Burton, Hetty

Ann Burton, David Early Burton, Elizabeth Craige Burton and Samuel Alfred
Burton. Ex: wife Elizabeth Burton. Wit: James F. Baylis, James Burton.

Page 292. Thompson, William, Sr. (Dagsborough) Will made: 23 November
1822. Proved: 5 July 1823. Son Elijah Thompson, one bed and furniture in
possession of Bull Earling. Son Truitt Thompson sow and sheep. Daughter
Elizabeth Dukes (married woman) bed and furniture. Daughter Hannah
Short (married woman) bed and furniture, Son Daniel W. Thompson, my
dwelling house and land at head of Indian River to Laurel town, containing
130 acres. Son William J. Thompson, horse, 4 pigs and harrow. Daughter
Letty C. Thompson, bed, furniture, cow, spinning wheel, ewe and lamb and
to remain at the house of her brother for safe keeping. Son Daniel,
remainder of estate. Ex: son Daniel M. Thompson. Wit: Rhoda Carey, Phobe
Thompson.

Page 293. Lacey, Spencer. Will made: 10 March 1818. Proved: 6 July 1823.
Wife Mary Lacey, all my estate during her widowhood, at her marriage or
death to 3 children, William B. Lacey, Delasaly F. Lacey and Sally E. Lacey.
To John N. Lacey one bed. Son, Delasaly F. Lacey, the plantation where John
Chippe now lives. Daughter Sally E. Lacey, the plantation where old Derecy
now lives. Ex: wife Mary Lacey and son Wm. B. Lacey (Ref) Wit: Wm. C.
Ennis, Absolum Rust, and William Magee.

Page 294. Owens, John. Will made: 10 May 1821. Proved: 11 August 1823.
Sons Jonathan and John Owens all my wearing apparel. The entire of my
estate to daughters: Elizabeth Annastacy Owens, Mary Langrel, Sinia Owens
and Nancy Griffith, and Hessy Griffith's five children. After appraisal and
division of land by George Polk and Purnel Tatman, Daughter Elizabeth
Coverdale's part to be sold and money given to her. Ex: Son-in Law Joshua
Griffith. Wit: John Carlisle, William Langrel.

Page 295. Howard, Comfort. Will made: 18 March 1823. Proved: 2
September 1823. Daughter Elizabeth West, brass clock and case, large
looking glass. Granddaughter, Comfort H. Brown, $40. Granddaughter Mary
Jane Howard, $30. Granddaughter Margaret Howard, $30 and my silver
shoe buckles. Grandson, John Howard, carpenter, (son of Samuel) $40.
Granddaughter Comfort Hill Howard. The rest of my personal estate to Son
Thomas 1/3 part, Daughter Elizabeth West 1/3 part other 1/3 between
children of Robert Howard, dec'd. Ex; Thomas Howard, Lewis West. Wit:
William Russell and David Walker.

Page 296. Spicer, Curtis, Dagsborough Hundred. Will made: 14 May 1823. Proved: 23
September 1823. To wife Roday, 100 acres bought of Joseph Morris, Sr. during her
natural life then to John Spicer. To Roday 11 acres bought from

heirs of David Green after her death to son John. Land Nanticoke Hundred to sons James, Peter (U21), William(U21). Son John to pay daughter Elon $100 at age 21. James to pay Sarah $100 at age 21. Ex: Wife Roday. Wit: Daniel Hudson, Jane Morris, Nancy Morris.

Page 297. Hitchens, Sr., Edmund. Will made: 8 March 1823. Proved: 14 October 1823. Son Edmend Edmund Hitchens, tract called "Point Lookout" and "Security Enlarged." Grandchildren of son Peter: Benjamin, Samuel, Dolly, Cotman, Martin. Land Broad Creek Bridge to head of Indian River to Daniel Melson's land. All the remainder of my estate to be equally divided between my son Edmund Hitchens, daughter Levinia Hitchens, daughter Barshaba Burton, and Polly Bradford. Ex: Son Edmund Hitchens. Wit: Wm Vaughan, John Melson, Stokley Boyce.

Page 298. Truitt, Jarman. Will made: 27 September 1822. Proved: 8 October 1823. Son Elijah Truitt, son Littleton Truitt, daughter Sarah Lewis, daughter Nancy Littleton, Son-in Law Nehemiah Jones, all to receive one shilling each. Son Jarman Truitt- rest of my estate. Son William Truitt, one shilling. Ex: Jarman Truitt. Wit: Thomas West, William R. (Phipins??) James (?).

Page 300. Murray, David. Will made: 21 September 1823. Proved 18 October 1823. Sons Caleb and Joseph and grandson Henry Oliver Barrow, right and title to a piece of "Cypress Swamp" known as "Freeman's Neglect." Daughter Sophia McCabe, Daughter Hannah Williams, Granddaughter Betsy Johnson. Granddaughter Louisanie Simpler. Sons: John, William Nathaniel and Sacker. Wife Roday Murray the use of all my personal estate. Ex: Son Sacker. Wit: Ebe Campbell, Wm. Campbell, Jr.

Page 301, Phillips, Jr. Richard. - Will made: 29 August 1823. Proved: 31 October 1823. Brother George Phillips, ½ the house and land in Laurel where he now lives, ½ of tract of land near Georgetown, ½ house and lot in Little Creek —where Cpt. Jonathan Cathell now lives. Brother Levin Phillips $325. Brother Jonathan A. Phillips $750. Brother Samuel Phillips $700. Nephew Richard Phillips Darby $500. Sister Nancy Twilley $700. Sister Sarah Darby $300. Sister Levina Phillips $500, and not her husband, if he should try to sue for the money, the legacy to be null and void. Sister Betsy Bennett $600. Ex: Brother George Phillips. Wit: James Derickson, James Twilley, Ephraim Vinson.

Page 302 Dickerson Jonathan, Broadkiln. Will made: 29 August 1823. Proved: 18 November 1823. Wife Elizabeth, as her dower all the rents and profits of the plantation whereon I now live, also the place where Peter Salmons now lives adjacent each other, also sufficient of my personal estate, on condition that she raises my son Molton, and gives him a good English education. Daughter

Elizabeth Dickerson, the land whereon Alexander Kimmey now lives, which I purchased of Elihu McCracken and James Redden 89 acres, also the land purchased of Eli Carpenter and Thomas Messick 30 acres. Daughter Amelia Dickerson, land where my brother Samuel lives in Nanticoke Hundred 200 acres, also ½ the land I hold with Richard Salmons, Nanticoke Hundred. If Richard Salmons collects the bond due me from William Jones, to myself and Richard Salmons, without expense to my estate, then I give that to my daughter Amelia. Son Alleson Dickerson, land I own in Cedar Creek Hundred Called ? Warren 250 acres, also all the land over the branch to the southern side of my plantation purchased from Brinkley Davis "New Ground," also part of "Old Isaac's Field." Son Molton (U21) all the land I now live on, also the place where Peter Salmons lives, after the death of my wife Elizabeth. Ex: Brother Peter Dickerson (refused) and my friend Jehu Stockley (refused). Wit. Job Smith, Jeremiah Wattson, and David Wattson.

Page 305. Morris Mary - Nuncupative Will Broadkill Hundred, declared by her word of mouth Monday 17 November 1823 at her usual place of abode. "That my will and desire is that Thomas Lank and his heirs shall have the whole of my estate and also that Thomas Lank shall settle my business as witness our hands this 19 November 1813." Proved: 1 December 1823. Wit: Reuben Miller, Naomi Morris.

Page 306. Russell, John (Broadkiln). Will made: 9 April 1823. Proved: 9 October 1823. Granddaughter, Comfort Lockwood, bed, furniture, walnut case of drawers, walnut dining table, pr large brass left hand Irons, looking glass, cherry tea table and $20 and 1/12 part of estate Granddaughter Jane Horseman Howard, wife of Thomas Howard, and daughter of my son John Russell, land in Lewes Rehobeth Hundred lying in the forks of the roads leading to the right by and through Quaker Town and to the left down into Rehobeth Neck. Part of a tract purchased of Comfort Prettyman (dec'd). 50 pounds which I paid William Harris towards building a house on said lands and 1/6 part of estate. Son Joseph Russell, house and land in Georgetown, on the Square, which I purchased of Peter Parker Harris, on condition that he pays for enhancements and repairs on the place... if he refuses then the property to be sold account against his for sash dated February 1806, Also, 4 Vol.'s of *Blackstone's Commentaries of-Law and Appendice* and book *Everyman His Own Lawyer*. Articles of agreement between myself and son William Russell 20 May 1811, I have conveyed unto Rhodes Shankland, now dec'd as assignee of my said son, all the tract of land in Broadkiln Hundred 240 acres, which I purchased of James P. Wilson, subject to the paying of 50 pounds to my grandson John Russell, son of William Russell, when he arrived at age 21. Daughter Ann Horseman Fassett, dec'd, late the wife of John R. Fassett, household goods in her possession, also 175 acres of land in Baltimore Hundred, adj. Lands of John R. Fassett, her husband. Four lotts in

Georgetown, which I purchased for William Russell to be sold and money divided among my 4 great grandchildren: Catherine and William Phillips Russell and my great-grandchildren David Lockwood and William Russell Lockwood, Children of my granddaughter Comfort Lockwood. William Russell Lockwood to receive my silver watch, which was formerly his grandfather Phillip Russell's. Grandchildren Matilda Horseman Melagoose and Matilda Rusel, the 1/6 part of my estate, equally divided. Granddaughter Jane H. Burton, 2 lotts fronting on Market Street in Georgetown, #200 and #201 on platt. Grandchildren namely: Nancy, John, Joseph and Elizabeth Evans, children of my daughter Elizabeth Evan (dec'd) $100 from money raised out of the money due me from William Russel for the purchase of the lands in Cedar Creek which were the lands of William Daniel. To son John Rusel all the lands purchased of William Jones and the McCalley's situated in Nanticoke Hundred, two lotts in Georgetown #190 and 192, If he dies, without heir, personal estate to be divided between the two daughters of William Rusel, Mary and Ann Rusel- his real estate To be divided between his sons Joseph, John and William Rusel. To my grandchildren, Jane H. Burton, Joseph, Mary, John, William, Ann and Matilda Rusel children of my son William all the lands in Broadkiln Hundred which I purchased from the Stuart's and Peter Parker Harris and my part of the "Beehive Swamp," however, son William is to sell the lands and the money be equaly divided between the above named children of his. Ex: Sons William and John Russell. Wit: M. Rench, G.A. Ewing, James P.M. Kollock.

Page 310. Draper, Maud. Will made: 30 August 1823. Proved: 9 December 1823. Wife Sally, the farm 220 acres during widowhood, also 2/3 of 130 acres of marsh bought of George Read. Sons Charles and Ratcliff, the three farms in Cedar Neck 600 acres divided between them. Son Alexander the land I own in Slaughter Neck, one farm adj. Lawrence Riley and Luke Lofland, piece of land that was formerly Hines and Farm purchased of Thomas Draper. To son Maud and Henry the lands where I now live and 2/3 of the marsh purchased of George Read at marriage or death of my present wife. Daughter Sally Heavelo, the house and lott I own at Milton and the land I own near south Milford. Ex: Wife Sally Draper and friend Thomas Draper (Ref). Wit: Henry Hooper, William Wilcocks and Sam Paynter.

Page 313 Short, Shadarack Sr., Broad Creek. Will made: 5 September 1811. Proved: 22 December 1823. Son Shadrack Short, land he lives on called "Agreement" bought of Gilbert Marriner and George Mitchell. Son Phillip Short, the plantation I live on called "Friendship" and a piece called "Addition" and "Downes Chance" Grandson Shadarack Short, son of Uriah, "Golden Lotts," purchased of Wm H. Walls and "Wooden Mind" with a division line with Aaron Collins. Son-in-Law William Anderson $50. Daughter Rhoda Hosea. 750 acres purchased of Wm. Anderson to be divided between daughter Vinea Lord, sons

John Short, Uriah Short, Isaac Short, Shadarack Short, Phillip Short,
Daughters Rhoda Hosea and grandson Shadrack Short. Ex: Son Phillip Short.
Wit: M. Derickson, Robert Wiltbank and Joseph Godwin.

Page 315. Tull, Chambers. Will made: 23 December 1823. Proved: 2
February 1824. Wife Mary 1/3 part money in hand. Sons: Richard Tull and
John Tull (Youngest), all the rest of my money. To Nancy Kirby $30.
Grandson Littleton Russell $19. Granddaughter Adeline Russell $10. My
moveable property, to sons Richard and John Tull. Wit: Laben Jones, Robert
Wallace and John Tull of Stoughton.

Page 315. Morris, Hezekiah. Will made: 2 January 1824. Proved: 3 February
1824. Son Carmen Morris $8. Son William Morris, $200, if he should marry a
certain Sara Ward (widow of John Ward) he is to receive 1 shilling in lieu of
above. Hamilton Ward, my grandson, $25, when he turns 21. Levin Morris
(alias) Andreus (U21) $25. Granddaughter Hananow Ward, bed, furniture
and cow. Son Constantine T. Morris all my lands including plantation. Ex:
Constantine T. Morris. Wit: Jeremiah Nicols, Isaac Jones, Samuel Laws.

Page 317. Marvell, Robert, Sr. Will made: 17 July 1817, Proved: 5 February
1821. To Robert Barr, all the land. Negroes Robert and woman to be free,
Negro man Fisher to be hired out or sold to someone in the neighborhood,
so he will not be sent out of state until he is 28. Ex: Wife Mary Marvell and
Purnal Tindal (both ref), recommend Robert Barr as Administrator. Wit:
John Tindal, Miles Tindal.

Page 318. Burton, James, Angola Neck. Will made: 29 June 1823. Proved: 9
February 1824. Wife Polly Burton, one plantation adjoining lands of Robert
Prettyman, Cord Burton and John Lingo and Ivy Branch, also the "Three
Islands" on Herring Creek. Son John Hamilton Burton, property divided by
my brothers Samuel and John Burton. Eldest son, James Burton, lands
purchased of George Robinson. Ex: wife Polly Burton. Wit: James F. Baylis,
Thomas Burton.

Page 320. Clark, Jacob A. (Baltimore Hundred). Will made: 2 January 1824.
Proved 1 March 1824. Mother Ede Coulter $1. Brother Wm Coulter, 25cents.
Brother George Coulter 25 cents. Sister Mary MeCullo, 25 cents. Wife Rhoda Clark
all my estate. Ex: wife Rhoda Clark. Wit: Ebe Walter, Pemberton Burton.

Page 321. Barker, Bagwell. Will made: 28 February 1824. Proved: 3 March
1824. Wife Polly N. Barker, tract of land called "Fishing Point," at her
marriage or death to go to her child that she now is pregnant with, if child
dies without heir then to my daughter Kitty Vickers and my son James L.
Barker. Wife

should have Negro Nathaniel and Negro girl Sarah during her widowhood then to the child she is now pregnant with, until they are 28 years of age, and then they are to be free. My wife Polly N. Barker should also have best bed and furniture, 3 cows and calves, best yoke of oxen, my ox cart, horse and carriage, plow and harrow, best weeding hoe, 5 ewes and lambs, best chairs, 2 best tables, one stand, looking glass, one of my best chests. Large iron pot, small iron pot, one loom and warping bars, one new carpet, 6 earthen basins, 6 earthen bowls, 100 bushels of corn, 500 weight of bacon, five bushels of wheat, 3 stacks of hay, three of fodder and $300 cash. If my wife marries or dies, then everything to my son and daughter. To son James L. Barker Negro boy George Burton until the age of 28 then he is to be free. To daughter Kitty Vickers, my Negro girl Susan until age 28 then she is to be free. That my son- in-law, Edward Vickers should have full privilege to move his house where he now lives and that Edward Vickers and James L. Barker shall move my storehouse anywhere they deem fit. The rest of my property is to be divided between Kitty Vickers and James L. Barker. Ex: Edward Vickers and James L. Barker. Wit: John Thoroughgood, James Starr, Samuel Lockwood, Jr.

Page 323 Lockwood, Mary, widow of Samuel. Will made: 8 June 1820. Proved: 6 April 1824. Granddaughter Mary Wilkins, wife of Elijah Wilkins, one calico gown. Mary Lockwood, wife of Benjamin Lockwood, one calico gown. My blackman George, to be free and the sum of $25. Joshua Robinson, Betty Long and Samuel Lockwood (my children) and Zipporah Lockwood, daughter of my husband Samuel. Ex: William Lockwood. Wit: Edward Dingle, William Howel.

Page 324. Thoroughgood, Miller. Will made: 5 March 1824. Proved: 27 April 1824. Wife Eleanore, 1/3 part personal estate, also 1/3 part of the home plantation and 1/3 part of timberland. Son Paul Thoroughgood, the plantation, whereon I now live. Two daughters, Sally Thoroughgood and Nancy Thoroughgood, all the lands I bought of Margery Willey and Phillip Short and wife, and so much of the survey made by John Willey and myself as belongs to me and such other lands as I may possess at the time of my death. To my daughter Sally Thoroughgood -$60. To daughter, Nancy Thoroughgood -$60. My personal estate to be equally divided between my 3 children Paul, Sally and Nancy Thoroughgood. Negro boy Daniel shall be free at age 28. Ex: wife Eleanore and Paul Thoroughgood. Wit: Ed Dingle, Jr., Ann Houston, John Willey.

Page 325. Taylor, Nancy. (Baltimore Hundred) Will made: 3 March 1824. Proved: 3 June 1824. Daughter Mary Ellis, my new corner cupboard, Daughter Sarah Lynch. Granddaughters Nancy W. Taylor and Mary R. Taylor, Sarah Lynch to take care of them until they are 18. Three grandchildren William J.

Taylor, Elizabeth Taylor and Mary Taylor $2 each. Son William, hogs, geese, gun and cow. To Grandson Lambert R. Taylor, my silver Watch. Estate to be divided between children Mary Ellis, Sarah Lynch and William Taylor. Son Elijah Taylor $1. Ex: William L Taylor and Sarah Lynch. Wit: Eber Long, Ebe Campbell, William Campbell

Page 326. Phillips, Samuel of Richard. Will made: 24 April 1824. Proved 11 June 1824. Brother Jonathan Baclay Phillips, the farm which was left to me by the death of my father Richard Phillips. Brother Levin, Brother George, Nephews John Twiford Darby (Father Thomas) and James Twilley. Sister Levinia Phillips. Sister Betsy Bennett. To brother Jonathan Baclay Phillips, Negro girl Eleanore that was bequeathed to me by my brother Richard, until she turns 21, then she is to be free. Ex: Brother Jonathan Phillips. Wit: Gideon Badley, Jonathan Bailey, and Samuel Moore.

Page 328 Wolfe, Daniel, Lewes - Rehobeth Hundred. Will made: 18 June 1823. Proved: 18 June 1824. Sons: Levins Milby Wolfe and Nathaniel Wolfe, Daughter Comfort Hickman. Son William Rufus Wolfe $100 per year to be paid annually out of the profits of my estate. Wife Mary Wolfe, my Negro woman Alice, best horse and gig. All the remainder of my estate, houses, lands to my four sons: Reece Wolfe, Daniel Wolfe, Joshua Wolfe and John White Wolfe, and my five daughters Elizabeth, Mary Ann, Sarah, Jane and Hannah White Wolfe. Friends Daniel Rodney, Caleb Rodney, Robert Burton (farmer) John Wiltbank to divide property between my 9 children. Codicil: Son Rufus or William Rufus should have one equal share of my estate. Levin Milby Wolfe to have one share divided in 1/2. Wife Mary, bed and furniture, over and above the legacies left. She should be entitled to dower. My Negro Men Jerry, Milfor and Ceasar shall be free. Ex: Wife Mary Wolfe. Wit: Robert Burton, Hanry J. Rodney, Daniel Rodney.

Page 331. Burton, Benjamin, Dagsborough. Will made: 2 June 1824-Proved: 22 June 1824. To my brother Miers Burton ½ of my upper Saw Mill and gristmill and ½ part of 20 acres which lays adjoining the mills. To nephew, Benjamin Burton, son of Daniel Burton, the other ½ of saw mill and grist mill and ½ of the 2 acres adj. Brother Miers, all my land which lay between his lands and the lands of Joshua Ingram (dec'd) on the north side of the road leading from the store owned by myself and my brother Miers, to the place commonly call "Ingram's Old Field." To nephew Benjamin, son of Daniel, all the land lying on the south side of a line drawn from the Indian Neck to the road the leads from the store, belonging to myself and brother Miers, what is called "The Old Landing" extending up to the lands of Wingate and Ingrams. Nephew John H. Burton (son of brother Daniel), ½ part of the saw mill and grist mills, standing on the Creek side called the lower mills-Also, all the lands lying on the north side of the road leading to the lands of Bell's Heirs up to the lands of nephew Benjamin's. Nephew Nathaniel, (son of brother Woolsey), my lands occupied by Phillip Short, consisting of three tracts of land. To brother Meirs, ¼ part of my tract called "Lebanon," My brother Woolsey Burton's daughters Mary Burton, Priscilla Burton, and Elizabeth Burton ¼ part of "Lebanon" each. (Brother Meirs shall occupy the land until Woolsey's daughters arrive of age or marry.) To brother's Woolsey's four children: Nathaniel, Mary, Priscilla and Elizabeth, ½ of a tract called "Plantation" in Long Neck, Indian River Hundred, which was purchased of brother John Burton. Nephew Daniel Burton, son of Brother Daniel, one tract of land in River Hundred bought of William C. Williams. David Burton, son of Daniel, tract of land purchased of Mary Hemmons in Indian River Hundred. Benjamin, son of Brother Daniel, tract of land known as "Burton's Island." To Brother John, - $2000 in cash. To clerk Jonathan Cottingham $100. To housekeeper, Polly Cobb, bed, furniture and $200. Aunt Hessy Hopkins $30. The remainder of my estate divided between Brother Meirs, Brother John, Children of Brother Woolsey, Children of Daniel Burton. Samuel G. Wright shall have the ore on my lands as contracted at $1 per ton. Ex: Meirs Burton. Wit: Edward Dingle, Jr., James Littleton, Sary West.

Page 335. Shockley, William — Will made: 9 August 1823. Proved: 29 June 1824. Wife Elizabeth, house and land that I have had re-surveyed by Lawrence Riley on 1 August 1823, being the lands on the East and west side of the county Road except ½ of the buildings and lot of ground where I now live, that I intend for my daughter Kitturah Shockley and ½ for Eliza W. Shockley. For my wife a percentage of the marsh in Slaughter Neck. Daughter Sarah Adkins (wife of Leonard) $200, also the house and lot in Milford and all the property and all the property already given her. Son George Shockley, part of my lands in Slaughter Neck, Also a part of woodland adj. William Hickman, George Bennet. Son Lemuel B. Shockley, $1000, also ½ of 48 acres of land in marsh in Slaughter Neck next to Son George. Daughter, Eliza W. Shockley, land and marsh on the north and east of a division line with my wife Elizabeth, formerly belonging to Joseph Haslett; also woodland bought of Joseph Hickman, adj. Maud Draper, ½ the lands after death of my wife. To daughter Kiturah, all the lands on west side of the old County road, ½ a lot on west side of Road, piece of woodland bought of William Hamblton, $200 left to her by her grandfather Levi Warren. Son William, land in Slaughter Neck, piece of land bought of Nutter Lofland adj. Land of Purnell Bennett, $200 left to him by her grandfather Levi Warren. Granddaughter Eliza W. Lofland (daughter of Amelia) $50. Grandson Alfred Lofland (son of Amelia) $50. Grandson Alexander Draper (son of Lydda) $50. Ex: Wife Elizabeth Shockley and sons George and Lemuel Shockley. Wit: Lawrence Riley, Samuel Hart, David Gray.

Page 339. Ludinum, Rosannah. Will made: 19 April 1824. Proved: 20 July 1824. Son, Purnal Layton. Daughter Peggy Allen. Daughter, Hessy Victor. Granddaughter Peggy Layton. Grandson Burton Layton. Grandson Burton Victor. The residue of my estate to daughter, Hessy Victor. Ex: Burton Layton and Wesley Victor. Wit: Jno Cary, Phelimen Boysman.

Page 340 Adkins/Atkins, David (Baltimore Hundred) Will made: 8 April 1824. Proved 3: August 1824. Wife Jane Adkins, all my moveable and personal estate, and land in my possession. Ex: Wife Jane. Wit Edward Dingle, Jr. George Truitt.

Page 341. Kollock, Phillips (of Georgetown) Will made: 23 June 1824. Proved: 2 July 1824. Wife Betty Kollock, bedstead and furniture and all silver plate she owned at our marriage which is now in my possession. My four daughters Hetty, (wife of Levin Stuart), Mariah Wright, Hannah, (wife of Jehu Stockley), Penelope Walton (wife of Paynter), all the rest and residue of my estate: with this special condition that Hetty Stuart pay into my estate $20. — if she fails to do so, the estate to be divided between my other three daughters. All of my real estate to be sold and divided among my four daughters. Ex: Jehu Stockley, Wit: John Handy, James Evans, Nancy Waller.

Page 343. Bloxum, John (Northwest Fork Hundred) — Will made: 16 November 1822. Proved: 24 August 1824. All my real estate at death to daughters Sally, Nancy, Peggy and Mahala Bloxom who are single. If two are married at time of my death, land is to be sold and divided between my 8 children: Levin, Kendal L., Sally, Nancy, Mahala, Polly Collins (wife of Jerimiah) and Phamey Cannon (wife of Matthew). First son or daughter of Jerry and Polly Collins to have my silver watch, which is to remain in the family. Ex: Son in law, Jerimiah Collins with my daughters Sally and Nancy (refused) Bloxom. Wit: John Gibbons and James L. Wallace.

Page 347. Hudson, McKemme - Will made: 16 Jan 1820. Proved: 31 August 1824. Wife Hannah, all my real estate and moveable property during her life, then as follows: Son Robert Hudson, all my land and house; Son McKemme Hudson, bed, furniture and sheep; Son William M. Hudson, if he should return to this place, one bed and furniture and sheep; Granddaughter Margaret Hall Hudson, bed and furniture at age 16, if she does not live to brother William M. Hudson. Six Children to divide rest of estate at death of their mother: Patty Janice, Tanny Hudson, Nancy D. Richards, Robert Hudson, McKemme Hudson, William M. Hudson. Ex: Son Robert Hudson. Wit: William J. Hall, Micajah Turner, and John Hall.

Page 348. Prettyman, Benjamin - Will made: 1823. Proved: 16 September 1824. Son Lewis Prettyman, tract of land and Plantation which was deeded to me by

70

my father Thomas Prettyman. Wife Elizabeth, all the other estate, real and personal — she to provide legacies to Grandchildren Lydia P. Prettyman, Jane J. Prettyman and Robert Prettyman, a bible worth $5. To each. Daughter Comfort Prettyman, Son Lewis Prettyman, Daughter Hetty Prettyman, Daughter, Patience Prettyman, and Daughter Elizabeth Prettyman. Grandson Benjamin, son of Lewis, land purchased of heirs of Lewis West. Ex: Elizabeth Prettyman. Wit: John Parker and Ann Parker

Page 349. Moore, William- Will made: 1821, Proved: 20 September 1824. Daughter Sally Jones (wife of William Jones) all the land I hold on northwest side of Turkey Branch and 1/3 part of Saw Mill. Son John Wesley Moore, the plantation where he now lives, 1/3 part of Saw Mill, Son Perry Bartini Moore, land purchased of Robert Hitch, where Joseph Ellis lived and died, 1/3 part of Saw Mill. Daughter Polly Irving Moore, land purchased from Thomas Moore, where Stephen Waller lives, with the exception of 50 acres which is to be sold. Son Isaac Walcock Moore, land where he now lives on easternmost side of Turkey Branch, bounded by lands Jacob Herin and lands late of Anthony Collins (dec'd) and lands of Charles Moores (dec'd) and on the southward by the lands late of Isaac Moore (the Elder, dec'd). Ex: Perry B. Moore. Wit: Henry Bacon, James H. Spicer and Lewis J. Mailes.

Page 355, Kinnikin, Waitman— Will made: 13 September 1824. Proved: 28 September 1824. Son Jonathan, tract of land formerly belonging to the Cook's, situated in Little Creek Hundred, adj. lands of Thomas Collins, Wm Collins, and James Hastings. Daughters Sarah Kinney (wife of Joshua Kinney) and Eleanor Kinney (wife of Samuel Kinney) land adj. Jonathan Kinnikin and James Hastings, Two younger daughters Priscilla P. Kinnikin and Rachel Kinniken, all the residue of Land. Ex: Joshua Kiny, Wit: Thos.Collins, James Hastings.

Page 356. Russell, Hester, Broadkiln Hundred. Will made: 13 June 1817. Proved: 27 August 1824. Son William Russell, bed, furniture, and silver teaspoons. Daughter Lydia, bed, furniture and silver Tablespoons (this was crossed out). Son Robert Russell $2. Ex: Son William Russell.
The line was stuck out and the item silver tablespoons, devised to Samuel and Elias Russell, sons of Robert Russell. Wit: Robert West, Lydia Davenport.

Page 357. Carpenter, Avice, Widow, Will made: 23 October 1824. Proved: 26 October 1824. Son Isaac Carpenter $12. Ex (refused). Son John Carpenter for 2 children-clothes. Granddaughter Avice L. Donovan bed and furniture. Granddaughter Jane L. Carpenter bed and furniture. To son Messick Carpenter cow and calf. Daughter Sally Donovan, heifer and balance of estate. Wit: William Pierce, Sr. and Elizabeth Pierce.

Page 358. Dingle, Edward Sr. - Will made: 10 December 1823. Proved: 20 November 1824. Daughter Betsey, sons, John and Edward Dingle, Jr. All my lands being on the northwestern most side of a line drawn from the border of "Poor Chance," A white oak by Paul Waples house to the beginning border of "Dingle's Inheritance," a (?) white oak, a line drawn along and with the south line of "Dingle's Inheritance" which will be south 38 degrees and 108 poles, variation to be allowed, and from the end of said south line thence with a line drawn to the southeasternmost corner of "Abigail Chance" the same said land lying on the northmost side of said three lines. I give to my son John W. Dingle, all my lands lying on the southeasternmost side of the above lines consisting of a part of "Poor Chance," part of "Dingle's Inheritance." Tract called "Groom's First Purchase." I give to my daughter Betsy Dingle; and after her death to my son Edward Dingle, Jr. Ex: Edward Dingle, Jr. Wit: Paul Waples, John B. Waples.

Page 359. Tharp, Benjamin — Will made: 14 October 1824. Proved: 28 November 1824. Wife Sappy Tharp, all my real estate, after her death to George Pratt and Henry Pratt, except $50 to William Sipple, and $50 to Louisa Pratt. Ex: Friend William Sipple and Wife Sally Harp(Ref) Wit: David McKnitt, David Taylor, Thomas Chane, Benaiah McKnitt.

Page 361. Vinson, Elizabeth (Little Creek Hundred) Nuncupative Will June 1.-Proved: 24 November 1824 "She wanted her grandson Joseph to have her chest and her grandson Miers to have her box that stood on the chest and her granddaughter Hetty to have $3. Her daughter Abigail to take her (key?) as her own." Witnessed 4 November 1825. Nancy English and Comfort Vinson.

Page 361 Joseph, Jeremiah, - Proved: 27 November 1824. Wife Unice 1/3 part of estate. Son Levin Joseph, all I advanced and $1. Daughter Sally Joseph, all I advanced and $1. Son Burton Joseph, all I advanced and $1. Daughter Elon Magee, all I advanced and $1. Son Samuel Joseph, all I advanced and $1. Son Noah, all my real and personal estate not already disposed of to my wife, after her death to be his. Daughter Nancy Johnson, all I advanced and $1. Daughter Mary Joseph, all I advanced and a maintenance from my son Noah provided she lives with him as part of his family — if she refuses then $1. Ex: Wife Unice Joseph and son Noah Joseph. Wit: Griffith Joseph, Mary Joseph and Betsy Griffith.

Page 363. Roach, William. Will made: 18 October 1824. Proved: 4 December 1824. To daughter Priscilla Roach, best bed and furniture, red cupboard, red chest, one case of drawers, one loom with 2 new stays, pewter plates. Remainder of my estate to be sold and money paid to Priscilla Roach when she comes of age. All with the direction of my dear friend Thomas Sherman. Ex. Bro Daniel Roach 1 shilling. Wit: Sarah Pollet and Henry O. Bennum.

Page 364 Truitt, John, Sr. Will made: 5 August 1818. Proved: 8 October 1824. Wife Anna — 1/3 of my home plantation, houses, orchard and lands and estate, during her natural life then to my son James Truitt. To son James Truitt the rest of my home plantation which is 2/3. To son John Truitt, the land I bought of Thomas Betts, where he now lives. Daughter Levinah Betts (married woman). Daughter Barsheba Hutson, bed, furniture, and large chest. Daughter Nelly Truitt. Ex: Sons John and James Truitt. Wit: Thomas Truitt and James Truitt.

Page 365 Hastings, Frederick. Will made: 13 November 1820. Proved: 9 December 1824. Son Peter. Wife Polly my land and all property during widowhood then to son Chela, he is to maintain my daughter Molly Hasting during her lifetime. Remainder of estate to maintain children living witn me, Emila, Betty or Billy, Nancy, Molly, Charles, Hetty, one Negro girl named Eliza to daughter Charlotte. Ex: Wife Polly Hastings. Wit: Levin Calloway, Elisha Parker.

73

INDEX

Gideon, 35; Henry, 60, 61; Hetty Ann, 61; Isaiah, 35; James, 61, 65; Jane H., 64; Jnu, 33; John, 50, 65, 68; John H., 6, 34, 67; John Hamilton, 65; John Hilliard, 53; Louisa, 61; Lydia, 35; Maria, 35; Mary, 35, 68; Meirs, 53, 68; Miers, 67; Nathaniel, 68; Patience, 61; Pemberton, 65; Peter Robinson, 53; Polly, 65; Polly Shepherd, 52; Priscilla, 68; Robert, 67; Samuel, 60, 65; Samuel Alfred, 60, 61; Sophia, 50; Thomas, 35, 65; William, 43, 49; William B., 35; Woolsey, 53, 68
BURTON'S ISLAND, 68
BUTLER, Benjamin, 25; Eunice, 25; Eunicy, 25; Jemima, 25; John, 25; Nancy, 25; Samuel, 25
BYRAN, Nancy, 1
CADE, Betsy, 6; John, 6; Samuel, 51, 58
CADE ADDITION, 2
CAKERS CHOICE, 47
CALHOON, Levin D., 14
CALLAWAY, Ann, 6; Benjamin, 5; Clement, 5; Ebenezer, 36, 37; Elizabeth, 5, 37; Ezekiah, 5; Isaac, 36, 37; Joshua, 5; Josiah, 37; Kendal, 5; Lowder, 32; Nancy, 5, 6; Nanny, 37; Nehemiah, 6, 36; Patience, 37; Rachel, 37; Sally, 20, 37; Sarah, 6
CALLOWAY, Eliza, .32; Joseph, 36; Levin, 12, 72; Unice, 5
CAMPBELL, Ebe, 29, 62, 67; John W., 60; William, 29, 62, 67
CANNON, ---, 49; Arcada, 14; Betsey, 16; Betsy, 39; Burton, 39; Catherine, 14; Charlotte, 8; Clayton, 15, 39; Clement, 8; Cyrus, 39; Ebenezar, 15, 16;

Edward, 43; Elijah, 14; Eliza, 46; Ennalls, 8; Esther, 31; Gibson, 39; Harriett, 14; Harriott, 32; Hester, 31, 57; Hudson, 8, 16; Isaac, 15, 16, 31, 46; Jacob, 15, 39; James, 8; Jeremiah, 8; Joseph, 8, 43; Joseph B., 39; Kitty, 8; Levi, 8, 16, 43; Levina, 31, 32, 39; Lucreatia, 8; Mary, 14, 39; Matthew, 69; Nancy, 8; Phamey, 69; Polly, 31; Priscilla R., 14; Risdon R., 40; Sally, 14, 43; Sarah, 40; Sylvester, 31; Thomas, 40; William, 15
CARD, Sarah, 34
CARD PLACE, 25
CAREY, Charles, 57; Comfort, 24; Eli, 24; Haslett, 24; Levina, 57; Polly, 56; Rhoda, 61; Thomas, 24
CARLISLE, Charles, 3, 29; J. Pemberton, 29; Joel, 13; John, 13, 18, 57, 61; Manlove, 10; Mary, 10; Nancy, 29; Pemberton, 29; Polly, 29; Priscilla, 29; Priscillah, 3; Rebecca, 29; Sally, 3; Thomas, 10; William, 13, 29
CARMEAN, Betsy, 36; Higgens, 36; Higgins, 36; Lovey, 36; Milly, 20, 36; Nancy, 36; Selah, 38
CARMEN, Polly, 10
CARPENTER, Avice, 70; Eli, 18, 63; Isaac, 70; Jane L., 70; John, 70; Messick, 70; Nebany, 55; Polly, 12; Rachel, 12; Rebecca, 45
CARR'S NECK, 32
CARRY, Joseph, 60; Woolsey, 60
CARY, Cornelius, 14; Eliza, 3, 14; Elizabeth, 14; Haslet, 24; John, 3, 10, 12, 25, 40, 69; Margaret, 14; Nehemiah, 3; Peggy, 14; Woolsey B., 38

Joseph, 17; Joshua, 50, 61; Kirone, 18; Moses, 18; Nancy, 61; Sally, 17, 18; Samuel, 17, 18; Sarah, 17; Selathiel, 17; Seley, 18; Seth, 27, 50; Turner, 50; William, 50; Zoan, 18
GRIFFITH'S LOT, 18
GRIMSHAW, George, 14
GROOM'S FIRST PURCHASE, 71
GULLETT, Eleander, 23; Ezekiel, 23; John, 1, 4
GUMBY, James, 49
GUNBY, Arroney, 52; David, 51, 52; Jacob, 51; Neomy, 51, 52; Stephen, 51
HADKINS, Sally, 28
HALL, David, 22; Eleanor, 60; Eliza, 22; George H., 1; Isaac, 38; John, 58, 69; Joseph, 9; Lemuel, 22; Maria, 60; Nancy, 3; Peter, 58; Sally, 22; Shadrack, 60; William J., 69; William Jordan, 22; William L., 58; Woolsy, 54
HAMBLETON, William, 60
HAMBLTON, William, 68
HAMMONS, ---, 45
HANCOCK, Peter, 19
HAND, Jane, 47
HANDERSON, Abram, 41; Elizabeth, 41; William, 41
HANDY, John, 14, 69; Sina, 19; Trustin, 19
HANE, Cornelius, 38
HANSHAW, Cary, 29
HANSON, Hannah, 33
HANZAR, Jesse, 45; Nehemiah, 45; William, 45
HANZER, Cary, 45; Comely, 45; Elizabeth, 45; Elwande, 45; Jacob, 45; John, 45; Nathaniel, 45; Peary, 45; Thomas, 45
HARDISTY, Salah, 1
HARGIS, Jacob, 4

HARMON, Ann, 29; Arge, 29; Ephram, 29; Nathan, 17; Sarah, 59; William, 29; Zadock, 17
HARMOND, Elie, 29
HARP, Sally, 71
HARRIS, Benton, 1, 48; Lovey, 18; Peggy, 22; Peter Parker, 63, 64; Robert L., 57; William, 37, 63
HART, Jane, 21; Samuel, 68
HARVEY, Sylvester, 44
HASLET, Joseph, 30
HASLETT, Joseph, 26, 68; Samuel, 24
HASTIN, Jonathan, 5
HASTING, Benjamin, 55; Daniel, 55; Eleanor, 28; Elihu, 28, 55; Elizabeth, 28; Henry, 55; Hesekiah, 55; Hezekiah, 28; Joshua, 38; Levi, 55; Levin, 28; Lydia, 55; Melvin, 28, 55; Michael, 55; Molly, 72; Obediah, 3; Rachel, 38; Relli, 55; Sally, 5; William, 28; Winder, 28; Winney, 55
HASTINGS, Betty, 72; Billy, 72; Charles, 72; Charlotte, 72; Chela, 72; Eli, 28; Elihu, 28; Emila, 72; Frederick, 72; Hetty, 72; James, 70; Molly, 72; Nancy, 72; Peter, 72; Polly, 72
HASTY, Ally, 16; Hetty, 16; James, 16; John B., 16; Polly, 16; Rachel, 3
HATFIELD, Mary, 59; Zachariah, 59
HATTER'S LAND, 1
HAYES, Charles, 1
HAYMAN, Fisher, 15; Isaac, 15; Martin, 15; Polly, 15; William Quinton, 15
HAYNS, David, 5; Mimey, 5
HAYWARD, Nancy, 2; William, 2
HAZZARD, ---, 1; Ann, 9; David, 1, 4, 15, 33, 35, 42, 60; George, 23, 37; Jacob, 54; Jane, 58; John, 51;

Lemuel, 2; Mary, 34, 53; Molly, 2; Nancy, 40; Simpson, 15, 51; Thomas, 5
HEARN, George, 36; Joseph, 36; Leviniah, 16; Polly, 37; Sally, 8; Samuel, 16; Thomas, 36, 55; W. Isaac, 28; William, 37
HEAVELO, Jonathan, 59; Sally, 64
HEAVLOE, Anthony, 33; Bennet W., 33; David, 33; Edward, 33; Jemima, 33; Jesse, 33; Margaret, 33; Mary, 33; Rhuben, 33; Stapleford, 33
HEMMAN, John Brereton, 44
HEMMONS, Anna, 45; John, 44; Mary, 68; Samuel, 30; Selah, 31; Thomas, 45; William, 44
HENDERSON, Benjamin, 57
HENNESS, Pegga, 21
HERIN, Jacob, 70
HEVELOES, Phillip, 50
HEVELOW, Phillip, 51
HICKMAN, Comfort, 67; Isaac, 23; Jacob, 23; James, 21; John, 23,56; Joseph, 68; Levy, 71; Mary, 22, 23; Michael, 23; Miriam, .22; Nancy, 22; Nathaniel, 56; Nicholas, 22, 23; Roger, 23; Sally, 23, 56; William, 26, 68; Zachariah, 23
HILL, Charles M., 24, 27; Elizabeth, 36; John, 7, 36; Levi, 6, 53; Prissilla, 50; Stephen, 15, 43, 58: Susanna, 32; Thomas, 39
HILLARDS MISTAKE, 2
HINES, ---, 64
HITCH, ---, 21; Isaac, 21; Levin, 37; Rachel, 38; Robert, 70; Samuel, 37; William, 37
HITCHENS, Benjamin, 62; Cotman, 62; Dolly, 62; Edmend Edmund, 62; Edmund, 62; Jarrett, 37; Levinia, 62; Lovey, 37; Martin, 62; Nicy, 30; Peter, 62; Peter D.,

30; Samuel, 62; Shaday, 20; Shadrick, 37; Spencer, 37
HOG ISLAND, 45
HOLESTON, Abigail, 25; Elisha, 25
HOLLAND, Albert, 14, 47; Aley, 28; Benjamin, 2, 22; Ebenezar, 54; Elisha, 53, 54; Elizabeth, 53, 54; James, 54; John, 4, 47, 53, 54; Joseph, 54; Magdalin, 54; Sophia, 58; Tabbitha, 54; Tabitha, 54; William, 54
HOLLAND'S ADVENTURE, 20
HOLLAS, Pegga, 21
HOLLAWAY, John, 2
HOLLIS, Demand, 21; Hinson, 21; John, 21; Lova, 21; Nancy, 21; Sylva, 21; William, 21; Zadock, 21
HOOD, John, 38; Mary, 38
HOOK, Naomi, 29
HOOPER, Henry, 64
HOPKINS, Hessy, 68; Jane, 33; John, 33; Leveniah, 33; Levin, 26; Tabitha, 4; William, 1
HOSEA, Rhoda, 64, 65; Thomas, 38
HOUNDS DITCH, 5
HOUSTON, Ann, 49, 66; Ann Laws, 49; Elizabeth, 35, 42; Isaac Howard, 49; John, 23, 49; John T., 49; Joseph, 35, 43, 49; Joseph Aydelott, 49; Leonard, 43; Liston A., 3; Mary, 43; Nancy, 43; Nottingham, 43; Polly, 56; Priscillah, 3; Robert, 43, 49; Robert Bell, 49; Sally, 43, 49; Sally Burton, 49; William, 35
HOWARD, Betsey, 56; Comfort, 61; Comfort Hill, 61; Jane Horseman, 63; John, 61; Margaret, 61; Mary Jane, 61; Robert, 61; Samuel, 61; Thomas, 61, 63
HOWEL, William, 66

MELSON, Betsey, 8; Daniel, 1, 62;
Elijah, 50; John, 1, 62; Mary
Ann, 14; Polly, 50
MESSECK, Asa, 30; Charlotte, 30;
Nathan, 30; Noah, 30; Sarah, 16;
William, 30
MESSECK'S CHOICE, 32
MESSICK, Amelia, .30; Covington, 4,
28; Elizabeth, 30; George, 26,
30, 49, 58; Hannah, 18; James,
9, 26,45; Letta, 24; Levi, 30;
Love, 30; Miles, 4; Minus, 30;
Nelly, 30, 58; Sally, 30; Samuel,
4; Sarah, 4; Thomas, 63; Willim,
30
METCAFF, Mary, 3; Thomas, 3
MIDDLETON, Jacob, 10
MILBY, Ann T., 48; Arthur, 46;
Benjamin L., 48; Levin, 48;
Nathaniel, 48; William P., 48;
William Prettyman, 48; Zadock,
48
MILL LOTT, 16
MILL SEAT, 59
MILLER, Drake, 48; Henry, 59;
Reuben, 63
MILLS, Jonathan, 33; Sarah, 33
MITCHEL, Aba, 15; John, 15; Sally,
15; William Clayton, 15
MITCHELL, Andrew, 19; George,
64; John, 18, 19, 56; Rhoda, 18,
25; Robert, 18; Thomas, 5, 6
MOORE, Benjamin, 47; Betsey
Idalit, 21; Charles, 21, 37, 47,
70; Charles Westley, 21; David,
44; Elijah R., 21; Elijah
Robertson, 21, 22; Elzey, 47;
Ester, 47; Garretison, 47;
George, 41; Gilley, 20; Hefty
Charity, 21; Isaac, 22, 70; Isaac
Walcock, 70; John, 20; John
Wesley, 70; Jonathan, 47;
Lauther Taylor, 21; Leonard,
47; Levin, 22; Louisa, 47;

Louther Taylor, 21; Lova, 47;
Luther, 47; Luther Layton, 21;
Matthew, 47; Milly Williams,
21; Nelly Rider, 21; Perry B., 70;
Perry Bartini, 70; Polly, 21;
Polly Irving, 70; Riston, 47;
Sally, 47, 70; Samuel, 67;
Tabitha B., 19; Terazy, 47;
Thomas, 70; Thomas T., 47;
Tincey, 47; Warren, 47;
William, 22, 41, 70
MOORE'S PRIVILEGE, 16
MOORES PRIVILEGE ENLARGED,
53
MORE, Thomas T., 41
MORGAN, Azepy, 23; Betsy, 25;
Elijah, 23; Francis Asbury, 23;
Hessa, 23; Jacob, 23, 56;
Lowrensey Dow, 23; Maggy, 23;
Westley, 23; William, 23, 32
MORRIS, Amelia, 51; Andreus, 65;
Anna, 1; Bebbins, 31; Bevens,
50; Burton, 27, 39; Carmen, 65;
Constantine T., 65; Eliza, 51;
Elizabeth, 47; Ephraim, 39;
Heavelo, 59; Hessy, 39; Hevalo,
31; Hezekiah, 65; James, 29;
Jane, 62; Jerimiah, 15, 36; John,
17, 39, 50, 51; Joseph, 29, 61;
Lacey, 24, 39; Levin, 65; Lidda,
29; Mary, 51, 63; Mitchell, 29;
Nancy, 62; Naomi, 63; Nicey,
27; Noah, 2; Polly, 27; Robert,
22, 27, 40, 50, 51; Sally, 29;
Sarah, 26, 50; Susan, 59;
Tabitha, 39; Thomas, 39;
William, 29, 30, 31, 36, 50, 51,
65; William M., 40; William R.,
59
MOSELY, Milly, 29
MUMFORD, Hannah, 44, 46; Isaac,
46; Jesse, 46; John, 26, 46;
Samuel, 46; William, 46
MURPHEY, Hannah, 37

MURPHY, Rachel, 21
MURRAY, Caleb, 62; David, 31, 62;
Elisha, 31; Isaac, 3 1; James, 31;
John, 62; Joseph, 62; Milbron,
31; Nelly, 31; Richard, 31;
Roday, 62; Sacker, 62; Soverign,
31; William Nathaniel, 62
MYSEC, Naomi, 45
NANCY FANCY, 24
NEAL, Arthur, 35; John, 35; Mary,
9; William, 35
NEEDLES, Nathaniel, 6
NEGRO, Abel, 17; Abraham, 18, 25;
Absolom, 4; Alfred, 42; Alice,
14, 67; Alse, 1; Arthur, 28;
Benjamin, 18; Betty, 10; Caesar,
13; Cato, 13, 56; Ceasar, 67;
Cleo, 25; Cloe, 24; Comfort, 14;
Cudjo, 40; Cuff, 18; Daniel, 9,
18, 25, 66; David, 43; Delia, 18;
Dennis, 10; Dinar, 45; Donney,
28; Draper, 17; Easter, 28; Edar,
42; Eden, 46; Eleanor, 10;
Eleanore, 67; Eliza, 72; Elzey,
54; Febea, 18; Fisher, 65; Frank,
26; George, 2, 18, 28, 66;
Hannah, 18; Hannan, 25; Harry,
39; Heriet, 28; Isaac, 18, 28, 42;
Jack, 28; Jacob, 1, 2; James, 28;
Jane, 14, 54; Jerry, 67; Joseph,
14; Laepool, 21; Leah, 19; Levin,
10; Lewezar, 28; Lizzy, 28;
Mahaley, 28; Major, 13; Mariah,
10; Mary, 13, 42, 43; Maryasa,
21; Maryatta, 28; Milfor, 67;
Milford, 4, 42; Milley, 10;
Moses, 9; Nance, 4; Nathaniel,
66; Nelly, 13; Parsley, 9; Peter,
28, 42; Phillip, 28, 54; Phillips,
21; Phillis, 28; Pompey, 4;
Rachel, 18, 25, 28; Robert, 4, 65;
Rod, 26; Rose, 42; Ruth, 33;
Ruthy, 14; Sampson, 2; Sarah,
28, 66; Susan, 66; Thamer, 42;

Thomas, 38; Tom, 26; William,
28, 42; Zadock, 2
NEIL, Robert W., 4
NEILL, John, 54; Robert, 53
NELMS, John, 55
NEW CHANCE, 8
NEW GROUND, 63
NEWBOLD, James, 1
NEWCOMB, Patience, 35
NICHOLSON, Theophilius, 36
NICKSON, Mary, 30
NICOLS, Jeremiah, 65
NUNEZ, Hannah, 33
NUNITZ, Daniel, 9
NUTTER, William, 43
OLD FIELD. 44
OLD .ISAAC'S FIELD, 63
OLD LANDING, THE, 67
OLD LUCK, 24
O'NEAL., Betsy, 10; Esther, 10;
Isabella, 10; James, 10; John, 10;
Judith, 10; Polly, 10; Rachel, 10;
Thomas, 10; William, 10, 36
OTTWEL, Drewilla, 44
OTTWELL, Betsy, 44
OTWELL,, Obed, 57
OUTTON, ---, 19; Ann, 32; Purnal,
32
OWENS, ---, 59; Elizabeth
Annastacy, 61; John, 61;
Jonathan, 61; Sinia, 61
P... RIDGE, 49
PALBATT, Samuel, 3
PALMORE, Unica, 47
PARKE, Comfort, 35
PARKER, Ann, 70; Elisha, 72;
Elizabeth, 34; George, 9, 34;
John, 9, 10, 34, 70; Joshua, 37;
Mary, 9; Peter, 9; Peter S., 55;
Rebecca, 10
PARMER, Jane, 30
PARMERS FOLLY, 50
PARRAMORE, Anarotta, 47;
Comfort, 47; Ebenezer, 47;

Lacy, 47; Mary, 47, Nancy, '47; Oing, 47; Peter, 47; Solomon, 47; Stephen, 47; Tabitha, 47; Unice, 47
PARSLEY LIKING, 57
PARTNERSHIP, 33, 42
PARY, Mary, 23
PAYNER, Cornelius, 9
PAYNTER, David, 9; John, 9, 44; Maritta, 9; Meritta, 9; Moses, ; Paris, 9; Richard, 28; Sally, 13; Sam, 64; Samuel, 4, 9, 13, 15, 55, 59, 60; Samuel R., 60; Thomas, 44; William, 4, 9
PENNWELL, Nancy, 21
PEPPER, Levin, 1; Wattson, 11, 29, 42; William, 2
PERRY.,---, 53; Harriot, 44; James N., 52; Jane, 38; Margaret, 58
PETTYJOHN, Ebcnezar, 47; Ester, 33; James, 47
PHILLIPS, ---, 49; Benjamin, 8; Betsy, 36; Burton, 33; Charles, 8; Elijah, 7; Eunice, 8; George, 36, 62, 67; Hannah, 69; John, 33; John Niclson, 8; John Sheppard, 33; Jonathan, 67; Jonathan A., 62; Jonathan Baclay, 67; Jonathan Bailey, 36; Joseph, 8; Leveniah, 36; Levin, 36, 62, 67; Levina, 62, 67; Levinah, 36; Levinia, 47; Major, 14; Nancy, 36; Peregrin, 36; Polly Wingate. 33; Reece, 59; Richard, 36, 62, 67; Samuel, 36, 62, 67; Sarah, 8; Spencer, 8, 26, 33, 39; Thomas, 8; Tindal, 47; Willy, 7
PIERCE, Elizabeth, 71; William, 58, 71
PINE GROVE, 32
PLANTATION, 68
POINT LOOKOUT, 62

POLK, Charles, 11; Elizabeth Ann, 11; George, 12, 41, 61; John, 36; Josiah, 44; Margaret W., 11; Peggy, 45; Robert, 5; Sarah, 3, 59; William, 1, 6, 36; William A., 59
POLLET, Sarah, 72
POND, Molly Johnson, 44
POOL, John, 25; Sally, 25
POOR CHANCE, 71
POPLAR RIDGE, 49
POTTOMACK ENLARGED, 8
POWELL, Ann, 43
POYNTER, Elizabeth, 21
PRATT, George, 71; Henry, 71; Louisa, 71
PRETTYMAN, ---, 45; Ann, 34, 59; Benjamin, 9, 12, 25, 41, 48, 70; Betty, 48; Burton, 57; Cannon, 48; Charlotte, 59; Comfort, 41, 48, 63, 70; Eliza, 59; Elizabeth, 6, 13, 70; Hetty, 41, 48, 70; Jacob, 1; Jacob W., 59; James, 34, 48; James H., 59; Jane J., 70; Jeames, 34; John, 3, 59; John C., 59; Joseph, 56; Levin M., 59; Lewes, 25; Lewis, 70; Lydia, 34; Lydia P., 70; Mary, 59; Matilda, 59; Nathaniel, 56; Patience, 41, 70; Peggy, 48; Peggy Cannon, 48; Perry, 56; Phoebe, 56; Rebecca, 56; Robert, 34, 65, 70; Robinson D., 13; Robinson Dashields, 13; Sally, 56; Sara, 59; Sarah, 34; Shephard, 56; Thomas, 6, 70; William, 15, 34, 48; Wingate, 6
PRICE, Benton, 20; George, 20; John, 20; Joseph, 20; Mary, 20; Nelly, 20; Robert, 20; Usua, 20
PRICKLEY PAIR ISLAND, 16
PRIDE, Job, 31; Rachel, 31; Woolsey, 1, 31
PRITCHARD, William, 7

ROUSE, Henrietta, 55; James, 55
ROWLAND, Isiah, 19
RUSEL, Ann, 64; John, 64; Joseph, 64; Mary, 64; Matilda, 64; William, 64
RUSSEL, John, 33; William, 64
RUSSELL, Adeline, 65; Ann Horseman, 63; Catherine, 64; Elias, 70; Hester, 70; John, 63, 64; Joseph, 37, 63; Littleton, 65; Lydia, 70; Mary, 31; Phillip, 64; Robert, 70; Samuel, 70; Thomas, 54; William, 31, 40, 61, 63, 64, 70; William Phillips, 64
RUST, Absolom, 36; Absolum, 61; Barney, 28; Clement, 6, 28; James, 28; Jerimiah, 28; John, 33; William, 28
SACK, Saru, 45
SAFETY, 49
SALMON, Benjamin, 44; Lucy, 44; Robert, 44
SALMONS, Annah, 44; Benjamin, 44; Betsy, 44; Mary, 56; Peter, 62, 63; Richard, 63
SALMONS ADDITION, 44
SAMMONS, Betsy, 44
SARNEL, John, 60; Sarah, 60
SCHOOL HOUSE FIELD, 1
SCOTTISH PLOT, 5
SDDR, Calda, 13
SECURITY ENLANGED, 62
SELBY, Zadock, 2
SELF DEFIANCE, 46
SEVEN LOTS, 26
SHANKLAND, Mary, 34; Rhodes, 3, 63; Sary, 34; William, 9, 34, 38
SHARP, ---, 17; Amy, 12; Clement, 57; Elisha, 57; Elizabeth, 57; Emaline, 57; Emeline, 57; Job, 12, 57; John, 17, 57; Nancy, 34, 57; Peter, 57; Phillip, 57; Rachel, 57; Sally, 12; Selby, 57; Thomas, 57; William, 12

SHAW, Sarah, 33
SHERMAN, Thomas, 72
SHOCKLEY, Curtis, 21; Elias, 3; Eliza W., 68; Elizabeth, 68; George, 68; Kitturah, 68; Lemuel, 68; Lemuel B., 68; Sarah, 68; William, 68
SHORT, ---, 49; Adam, 27, 31; Betsey, 27; Betsy, 25, 26; Daniel, 26, 27; Edward, 48; Eleanor, 48; Elizabeth, 12, 49; Elizabeth M., 49; George, 12; Gilly, 27; Gilly G., 26, 27; Hannah, 61; Henry, 12; Isaac, 15, 16, 27, 48, 52, 65; Ishmael, 1; James, 1; Jehu, 52; John, 1, 12, 26, 65; John Wingate, 26; Leonard, 26; Levina, 12; Mary, 12; Myranda, 48; Nancy, 12, 26; Nelly, 26; Neomy, 26; Phillip, 12, 48, 64, 65, 66, 68; Prissey, 26; Sally, 26, 52; Shadarack, 26, 64, 65; Shaderick, 48; Shadrack, 12, 64, 65; Solomon, 19; Uriah, 64, 65; W. Uriah, 18; Wingate, 26; Zipporaugh, 52
SILVER BANKS, 38
SILVER PLAIN, 57
SIMPLER, Louisanie, 62
SINCERITY, 10
SIPPLE, William, 71
SIRMAN, Job, 12; John, 12; Nancy, 12; William, 12
SKELLY, John, 38
SKINNER, Eleanor, 30
SMALL HOPES, 8
SMITH, B., 11; Charles, 32; Constantine, 31; Daniel, 32; Eli G., 26; Eliza, 60; Elizabeth, 45; Henry, 60; Hezekiah, 32; Job, 63; John, 11, 60; John D., 60; Joseph, 18; Josiah H., 60; Lovy, 32; Mary, 9, 45; Mary C., 60; Mathias, 19; Nancy, 24; Polly,

* 9 7 8 1 6 8 0 3 4 6 3 4 3 *